A Brand New You

The Ultimate Guide for Quitting Porn and Self-Transformation

Greg Strattner Jr.

The information contained in this text is not intended, nor implied, to be a substitute for professional medical advice. It is provided for educational purposes only. Always seek the advice of your physician or other qualified healthcare provider before starting any new treatment or discontinuing an existing treatment. Talk with your healthcare provider about any questions you may have regarding a medical condition. Nothing contained in this text is intended to be used for medical treatment or diagnosis.

ISBN 978-1-7321489-0-1 (paperback)

ISBN 978-1-7321489-1-8 (e-book)

Dedicated to those suffering in silence –

With perseverance you will prevail.

Table of Contents

Acknowledgements

A special thanks to my parents, and my sister, for always supporting me unconditionally in the pursuit of my dreams.

Preface | My Mission

"I cannot teach anybody anything,
I can only make them think."

Socrates

My mission is to provide you with direction, guidance, and a plan for how you can quit porn for good, and fast track the transformation of your ever-evolving self. A book is a lens to view the world through. This book is my lens. What I reveal in the coming pages is meant to make you think. These insights have been realized through my extensive experience, introspection, and self-analysis. What you do with these insights is completely up to you. However, I hope that my work will inspire you to test out these ideas for yourself, because it's ultimately you who must take the action needed to improve yourself and your life. Regardless of what happens from here on out, if you take nothing else from this book, I hope that you at least begin to think for yourself, if you haven't already started. I'm grateful for you, and I wish nothing but the best for you and your life.

PART I: The Awareness to Inspire

"Awareness is the greatest
agent for change."

Eckhart Tolle

CHAPTER 1

Seek Your Truth | A Reflection of Clarity

"Truth is by nature self-evident. As soon as you remove the cobwebs of ignorance that surround it, it shines clear."

Mahatma Gandhi

This text is a collection of the truths that I have discovered on my journey of self-transformation. I believe that each of us, through much mining and searching, have the ability discover our own set of truths. I believe that the only way to make this discovery is to go deep within ourselves, and to seek them out. Knock on the door, and the door shall be opened. I've learned that the fruit that is bared through the discovery of truth, is that of profound clarity and a deepened meaning for life.

I crawled through the mud for years in the process of uncovering these insights. Doing so has changed my life in so many positive ways. Sure, this journey hasn't been all sunshine and roses. It's been extremely hard at times.

Transformation often gets worse before it gets better. I always remind myself in times of adversity, that the ball has to hit the ground before it bounces back up, but when it does bounce back up, it will go higher than you could have ever otherwise imagined. It is in the times of difficultly and suffering where our strength and resolve is forged. Just beyond the pain, struggle and suffering lies the treasure. It is in this battle with everyday resistance that leads to the active realization of our full potential.

The potential that lies within each of us is immeasurable. Our efforts to realize this potential is a never ending process. Self-transformation has no final destination, and there are no limits to our personal evolution. The only limits we have are the limits we impose on ourselves. Without self-imposed limits, there's no telling what we can achieve, and who we can become.

That said, this book is not written to prove any specific point, although at times it will be very clear what my opinion is. This book is a tool for guidance, support, and clarity for those seeking their own truth, and the realization of their full potential. Everything I share with you comes straight from my heart. I've put my blood, sweat, and tears onto these pages, and I hope that my efforts will provide you with valuable insight that you can utilize on your quest for truth and self-transformation.

CHAPTER 2

The Deepest Meaning | A Brand New You

"The privilege of a lifetime is
to become who you truly are."

Carl Jung

What does becoming *A Brand New You* mean? While I cannot describe specifically what this means for you, as we all are unique in our own special ways, I can say that becoming *A Brand New You* is becoming a person who lives life in full expression of their authentic self. This means that you live every moment of every day to the best of your ability, as an expression of who you are at your deepest level. You live literally as a gift to the world, spontaneously and purely, as your own unique expression of light and love.

I also cannot tell you who you are on your deepest level. Only you can discover your authentic self through choosing to take full responsibility for your life. I also suggest that the door that leads to the discovery of who you really are at your core, swings inward. The key to opening this door to truth is to go within. And only from turning your focus inward, will you be able to recognize and peel back the many layers of conditioning that have accumulated during your lifetime.

Peeling off these layers of conditioning is like peeling an onion. As we progress through life, our experiences cause these layers of external conditioning to add up. The accumulation of these layers often cause us to lose touch with who we are at our deepest level. With each layer added, this connection to our authentic self grows weaker, and weaker. This process can go on and on until we get to the point where we don't even know who we are anymore.

Nearly all of the experiences that weaken this connection to our authentic self are influenced by external factors, norms, and societal expectations. If we are not conscious of this process, we allow ourselves to be completely at the mercy of the external world. This persistent external conditioning then leads to poor mental, physical, and spiritual health. Then as our health in each of these areas decline, we lose the ability to express who we are on our deepest level.

Another problem with the accumulation of these unnecessary layers, is that they block us from being able to feel deeply into both our own emotions, and the emotions of others. The inability to feel into both ourselves and others simultaneously, creates all sorts of problems in our life that can negatively affect our relationships, career, health, and our overall personal well-being.

However, as we become fully aware of what's going on, and begin to consciously take initiative to shed these unnecessary layers of conditioning, we get closer and closer to rediscovering who we really are at our core. Through this process of sorting ourselves out, the discovery and expression of our authentic self happens naturally, and effortlessly. The ability to live life freely as an expression of our ever-evolving authentic self is our ultimate goal.

CHAPTER 3

The Silent Assassin | Awareness of the Elusive

"Balk the enemy's power; force him to reveal himself."

Sun Tzu

The thickest, toughest, and most elusive layer of external conditioning to peel off is accumulated through the use of high-speed internet pornography. I've learned first-hand that porn use has a tremendously negative, but hard-to-notice impact on the mind, body and spirit. Most of the time, porn users don't even realize that it's their porn use that's causing a negative impact on their well-being, and how they feel.

This connection between the cause (porn) and symptom (negative affect) is often only realized once the cause is completely removed for an extended period of time. Porn is unique in this way because unlike other vices such as cigarettes or alcohol, which can be linked to obvious negative outcomes such as lung cancer, smoker's cough, and day-long hangovers, porn's negative impact is rooted below the surface of conscious awareness. Much of the negative impact is subjective, and cannot be quantified purely with numbers or data. Besides extreme red flag symptoms like porn induced erectile dysfunction, nearly all of the negative impact from porn use is intangible. The porn user just straight up feels terrible, and has no clue why.

Porn is like a silent assassin, slowly but surely killing our ability to feel authentic freedom, abundant joy, and unconditional love. It's like a tiny, hidden hole on a large boat, where if not fixed, will without question eventually cause the boat to sink.

The good news is that all of the real life damage that plagues porn users can be reversed by quitting. However, quitting porn is easier said than done. That's where this book comes in handy. This book is your guide for fixing this problem. Within these pages lie a collection of insights written in memoir format for the purpose of improving your quality of life. My goal is to help you enhance your life experience through the re-discovery and expression of who you are on your deepest level, far beyond the vice grip of internet porn.

By implementing the mindsets, strategies, and habits that I share with you in the coming pages of this book, you will be well equipped with the knowledge and understanding to successfully quit internet pornography for good, as well as discover what it means to live life as an expression of your authentic self. I have condensed my relentless approach to self-transformation into simplest form for easy comprehension and digestion. I have broken this process down into three main parts; *awareness, action, and attitude.* Mastering each of these areas is the key to self-transformation.

By using these insights on your own journey to freedom, I hope to save you a lot of time, effort, and contemplation; and in turn fast track your progress for achieving lasting positive change. I've dedicated thousands of hours of my life to refining and optimizing this lifestyle-system, so that you can become *A Brand New You.*

CHAPTER 4

Life on Rock Bottom | The Old Me

"There is no education like adversity."

Benjamin Disraeli

I begin by making the assumption that you, or someone close to you, is addicted to, or regularly uses internet pornography. Or maybe you're just curious as to what your life experience would be like without internet porn. Regardless of where you stand on the spectrum of porn use, I commend you for taking steps towards making positive change in your life.

When I eliminated porn from my life, I had no idea how drastic the changes would be. Quitting porn and rebuilding my life was the most important decision I have ever made. That said, I've learned that there's tremendous value in quitting porn. For me, quitting was a major step for reclaiming my personal power, freedom, and ability to love deeply. Take a moment to be proud of yourself for keeping an open mind, and exploring the possibilities of a better life. Driving toward change without certainty takes courage.

I won't bore you with my past, and to be frank I'm not one to dwell on the past, because I believe that it really serves very little purpose. Dwelling on the past is a great way to breed and harbor feelings of negativity. Living in the past causes us to cling to who we once were, and this clinging blocks us from being able to be who we want to be right now. I view life as a never-ending dance of change. Everything is always changing: seasons, weather, thoughts, emotions, feelings, and so on. It's important to be able to understand life from this perspective because by realizing this, we can then proactively influence this inevitable change with the intent of making it a positive one.

Heraclitus summarized this best in his quote, "No man ever steps in the same river twice, for it's not the same river and he's not the same man." The reality of constant change keeps a world of possibilities open to us. The power of change lies in the now. The present moment is where we can access this power and use it to our advantage. The present moment is where we find the key for improving ourselves and our lives. We will explore this concept deeper in the coming pages. As for right now, it's important to take a moment to share with you who I once was.

While I don't consider myself as ever being addicted to internet pornography, there was a span in my life of five years where I used porn 4-5 times per week. It's no coincidence that these years were the most miserable, self-destructive years of my life. But once I quit, my life changed profoundly in a relatively short period of time. My story is proof that you don't have to be addicted to porn to see major positive changes from quitting. Even if you are a casual user, you'll still find great value in eliminating this habit from your life. However, if you're suffering from a more extreme porn addiction, don't fear. Even the most demoralizing and crippling side effects caused by extreme porn use can be alleviated by quitting. That said, we all have a lot to gain from quitting our use of porn.

For the first 20 years of my life, I lived an adventurous and dream-inspired lifestyle. I was very proud of the person I was, as well as the direction my life was headed. I was super-social, outgoing, optimistic, and eager for what life had in store for me. I had big dreams of becoming a professional golfer, and playing on the PGA Tour. I had dreams of winning major championships. I had dreams of competing against the best golfers in the world. I had experienced love, and I had lived life as an expression of passion, captivation, and wonder. During this time period, porn was not a part of my life, and my life experience reflected this fact.

I started my quest to quit porn in February of 2015 at the age of 25. For the years prior to quitting, everything in my life looked fine on the outside. I had my life together for the most part. I had a good job, a steady social life, and I would have told you I was content with my situation had you asked me how things were going. But on the inside, my self-confidence, self-esteem, and optimism had been completely whittled away. Everything on the outside looked okay, but my interior was in ruins. My misery continued to persist, and I didn't have any idea why. Deep down, I felt helpless. I was doing everything that I was "supposed" to do, but why did I still feel so lost? I rationalized by telling myself that how I felt was just a product of doing what I was supposed to do. Because of this misunderstanding, I accepted how I felt because I thought that it was the "normal" way to live and feel. It turns out just because something seems normal doesn't mean that it's right. I learned this the hard way. "Living the dream" as many call it, was anything but that.

During the height of my porn use, the biggest red flag for me was the fact that my love life had completely evaporated. It was gone and nowhere to be found. Its disappearance baffled me. Where I once felt like I could attract whomever I wanted, I found myself powerless, hopeless, and confused. Another scary realization was that I had also lost my ability to feel a strong attraction to real women. I knew that I should feel attracted, but actually feeling the attraction seemed impossible. It made absolutely no sense to me. I couldn't understand why I always felt so damn empty. I had been in romantic relationships in the past, and I knew what love felt like, but I had no idea where my desire had gone. I had no clue why I felt the way I did. I was lonely, and I was in a very dark place.

And while I was financially secure at the time, I was working a job with no sense of fulfillment. I dreaded work. I was simply working to pay bills. I was just going through the motions, and I had become the definition of mediocre. I also didn't give a crap about much of anything. The scariest part of the entire situation was that I knew that I didn't care, but I didn't care that I didn't care. I was stagnant, and pessimistic. I wasn't going to the gym and working out anymore. I wasn't living out my passion for competitive golf. I wasn't setting goals or planning my future. I wasn't doing anything but causing suffering in my life. In a sense, I had given up on myself.

My motivation was also at an all-time low. I started to believe that my life experience was at the complete mercy of the external world. I felt like everything was completely out of my control. This powerlessness led me to continuously attempt to self-medicate in hopes of escaping reality. Because of this persistent escapism, I developed a slew of bad habits.

One of the bad habits that I adopted was binge drinking. I drank as often as I could physically handle, usually at least three times per week. When I wasn't drinking, I was recovering from it. I was a mess. During this same time period, I also developed a chronic marijuana addiction. I did everything high. I couldn't function if I didn't smoke. I even sold marijuana on a small scale to support this habit. My life revolved around my next smoke. Smoking also made me socially awkward. Because of this, I did my best to avoid social situations, and I strived for isolation. I was living in a state of perpetual fear, brain fog, and escapism. I was chained by my ignorance, and caged by my desire to escape. I was trapped. I was living life on rock bottom, and it all stemmed from my internet porn use.

Once I quit using internet porn, I was amazed at how all of the other bad habits fell out of my life effortlessly. Porn was like a tree, and the other bad habits were the branches that stemmed from this tree. It wasn't until I cut the tree down that I was able to dramatically transform myself and my life.

I no longer have any addictions, and life has become effortlessly pleasant. I attribute this transcendence to the relentless removing of the bad and implementing of the good. Removing porn and rebuilding my lifestyle has been similar to a country who removes a dictator from power. After the dictator is removed from power, the city must be rebuilt. It takes time, patience, and a sound strategy to rebuild the city efficiently and effectively. Rebuilding a life is no different.

As I reflect on this memoir of insights, I've been porn-free for the better part of three years, and life has never been better. Over time, I was able to transform from an immature, fear-driven grown boy; to an unconditionally-loving man, whose actions are derived from a place of pure joy, wonder and love. By utilizing these same insights in your own life, you too can be liberated, and achieve lasting self-transformation.

(NOTE: Anytime that I refer to "porn use" in this book, I'm also referring to masturbation. Porn and masturbation are closely linked. Keep this in mind for the remainder of your reading.)

CHAPTER 5

A Collective Cry for Help | An Advancing Problem

"The solution to adult problems tomorrow depends on large measure upon how our children grow up today."

Margaret Mead

In September of 2017, a cry for help hit me like a ton of bricks. I had just begun a YouTube channel, *Your Best Self Now,* which focuses on the many ways that we can design our lives for personal greatness, and learn to show up in life as the best version of ourselves.

I had always enjoyed using YouTube to learn new things, and expand my knowledge and understanding. I had wanted to create a YouTube channel for many years, and with the encouragement of one of my best friends, I finally built up the courage and took action.

I had reached a point in my life where I knew that I could help a lot of people by sharing what I had learned during my journey of self-transformation. I felt that to withhold what I had learned would have been selfish. Therefore, I started creating and posting videos on a daily basis. What started out as a hobby has now blossomed into what I know is my purpose in life.

The first video I ever posted was really bad. But somehow, it gained tremendous traction and began to go semi-viral. What was most interesting, was that the overall message of this video was about how much better my life had become since choosing to quit using internet pornography.

In this video, I shared how my decision to quit porn had dramatically improved my self-esteem, increased my self-confidence, boosted my libido, revived my dating life, deepened my relationships, and improved my emotional awareness of both myself, and others. I couldn't believe the response I received from viewers. Gratitude poured in by the thousands in the comment section.

It didn't seem to matter that the video had poor picture quality, was vertically recorded, had extremely vulgar language, continuous rambling, and was recorded from inside my car in the Home Depot parking lot. It still blew up. In fact, I find it hard to watch this video without cringing. Regardless, it was eye opening to experience the demand for this type of porn-quitting content.

At the time of this video upload, I had 0 subscribers. Fast forward to 7 weeks from the initial post, and from a statistical standpoint, the video had amassed over 85,000 views, 2,700 likes, 1,500 comments, and was viewed in every country in the entire world. I was amazed considering I had no following at the time.

So I continued on making videos every day. Many of these videos focused on answering specific, individual questions from viewers. I varied the topics of discussion, but I found out quickly that the videos where I shared strategies to overcome porn use were superiorly popular. These porn conquering videos outperformed all of my other self-transformational videos so consistently that it became alarmingly obvious that porn use was a large, actively growing cross-culture problem.

To put this into perspective, only 35% of my viewers are from the United States. These people are consistently looking for help, support, and guidance in any way that they can. I can feel their desperation in the hundreds of comments I receive every day.

This overwhelming cry for help has lit a fire within me that's hard to describe. With this urgency in heart and mind, I'm determined to do whatever I can to help those struggling with the same issues that I once battled with. I'm determined to lead as many people as I can toward achieving inner peace, and liberation.

Through mentoring hundreds of men through this world-wide platform, I've gained a great understanding for what specific issues these guys are struggling with, as well as their most frequently asked questions.

It's also very clear to me that we're now in a race against technology. As technology continues to advance, this problem continues to grow. The negative effects of internet porn use are now just emerging. Traditional research and modern medicine has fallen so far behind, and it's up to us to bridge this gap.

With persistent efforts to increase the awareness of this problem, the dangers of porn will become common knowledge. And as the impact of porn on our lives becomes common knowledge, there will be a wider range of helpful resources made available to those in need.

Porn use is a cross-cultural issue that cannot be ignored, nor taken lightly. We can't afford to wait for the cavalry to come and save us. We have to take the responsibility for solving this problem into our own hands, right now.

CHAPTER 6

Talking Taboo | Exposing the Avoidable

"The secret of freedom lies in educating people, whereas the secret of tyranny is keeping them ignorant."

Maximilien Robespierre

A major problem is that internet porn use is a topic that no one wants to talk about. It's that dark, secretive topic that everyone avoids at all costs.

Being addicted to something like internet porn causes an extreme type of shame and guilt. Accepting that you have the problem of being addicted to internet porn is a tremendously hard fact to first realize, and then to accept. This shame and guilt leads people to seek out help and guidance where they can remain anonymous. They fear being personally exposed, and act incognito to save their sense of self and protect their identity. We can't allow these people to suffer in isolation any longer.

This world-wide cry for help has been my primary motivation for taking massive action in providing an outlet on YouTube where people can come to for unbiased help, free of charge. However, we need to catalyze solutions on a much grander scale. I believe that it's important for us to have a much broader, long-term vision for solving this problem.

The most essential ingredient for this much needed shift in collective consciousness, is our ability to raise the awareness through active communication. We need to bring awareness to the dangers of porn use, and stop the silent suffering by talking about it.

For example, adolescents in sex education classes are taught that masturbation is "healthy". The problem with this, is that the dangers of porn use aren't included in this conversation.

This means that young adolescents, whom are at crucial stages in their development, are subject to the negative effects of exposure to pornography through pure chance. Because they are told that masturbation is safe, healthy and natural, they end up assuming that pornography falls into this same category.

Combine this misconception with how uncomfortable it is for a teenager to ask his teacher or his parents about porn, and it's almost guaranteed that the teen will choose to remain silent. This disconnect is extremely dangerous because without the proper awareness, these young people have virtually no way to pinpoint the root causes of the problems that inevitably manifest in the wake of porn use.

This is just one of the many ways of how we look at life that need to be adjusted in proportion to the degree of advancing technology. Sure, exploring our sexuality is important, but provided we do so in a healthy manner.

There's absolutely no argument that high-speed pornography is in any way healthy for exploring sexuality. In fact, I argue that porn portrays a false perception of what love is, and also creates unrealistic expectations of real life sexual interactions. Porn use also leads to the objectifying of women all together, which is a reality that must be stopped.

The fact that very few people are talking about this unhealthy sexual conditioning is incredibly disturbing. In fact, I argue that our overly sex-driven, sex-focused society is precisely the root of many of the problems in the world today.

With the increased popularity of high-speed internet pornography, and persistent exploitation of sex in the media, the importance of morals and values have diminished. The evaporation of these morals and values have resulted in a modern world that is more dysfunctional, violent, lustful, and polarizing than ever before. I don't believe that this is just a coincidence.

The truth is that internet porn is incredibly damaging to the brain. With prolonged use, porn can cause extreme problems such as but not limited to: porn-induced erectile dysfunction in men under the age of 30, the development of unnatural sexual fetishes such as straight men watching gay porn, and even catalyzing conditions such as chronic depression and anxiety.

The majority of the research of how porn affects the brain and the reward system has been conducted less than a decade ago. Traditional research practices function at a snail's pace compared to what is required to keep up with the speed of this technologically driven problem. We have to act, and we have to act now.

If you're skeptical, go explore the thousands of first-hand accounts of people who are sharing their experiences online. A great place to start is by checking out my YouTube channel, *Your Best Self Now*. The testimonials don't lie. This is a problem that can't be neglected any longer. We must act immediately because we're competing with the speed of the advancement of modern technology. We must address this before it cripples an entire generation of young people.

It's also important to note that I'm not a research scientist. I am a practitioner. I have successfully quit using porn through experimentation, self-awareness, and self-analysis. However, much of what I practice is based on proven science.

The point is that we are learning that porn is more dangerous than we could've ever imagined. The point is that there are thousands and possibly millions of people in the world that are being smothered, and paralyzed by this "new" problem. High speed internet porn is an extremely new concept when compared to the timeline of human evolution. Our brains are not equipped to deal and cope with the effects of what happens when we watch internet porn.

If you're interested in learning more about the scientific evidence and research behind how porn affects the brain, I highly recommend looking into the work of Gary Wilson. He's the author of an incredibly fascinating book, *Your Brain on Porn.*

CHAPTER 7

Stress and Porn | The Negative Loop of Escapism

"Problems are not the problem;
coping is the problem."

Virginia Satir

Life is stress. How we deal with the daily stresses of life greatly influence our well-being and happiness. If we allow ourselves to become overwhelmed, we often seek out ways to numb the discomfort, or to escape the pain that stress creates.

This escapism leads us to adopt many bad habits, such as drinking, gambling, over-eating, smoking, or using porn. All of which make us feel worse in the long run. This process of stress, escape, stress, escape, and so on; is a negative loop that prevents us from experiencing life in a free, joyful manner. In fact, the stresses of life are not all bad. It's only when we become overwhelmed with stress that we attempt to escape.

There are two kinds of stress that we experience as humans; positive stress and negative stress. In order to make our recovery from porn use as easy as possible, our overall goal is to minimize negative stress through focusing on the maximization of positive stress, but balancing this maximization with conscious rest.

Positive stress is the type of stress that we experience when taking on a challenge or added responsibility. This type of stress brings excitement, fulfillment, happiness and accomplishment into our lives. It feels good. It energizes us, and plays a crucial role in our personal growth.

Positive stress is what we experience when we go to the gym to work out, take our dog on a run, do yoga, or play a game of baseball. It also can be felt when we take on more responsibility at work, commit to writing a book, or starting a new business. Positive stress can even improve our performance in various aspects of our lives. However, this positive stress must be balanced with conscious rest, to keep it from turning into negative stress.

The unfortunate fact is that a majority of people are dominated by negative stress. Negative stress is birthed from a lack of life balance, combined with persistent overwhelm. We're living in a time where we have more responsibilities than ever before. It's easy to become overwhelmed when we're being pulled at from so many different angles, all at the same time.

Many people don't have the adequate habits and attitude in place to deal with stress effectively. This causes them to fall victim to overwhelm, which in turn creates and fuels negative stress.

Negative stress drains our energy reserves. It also decreases the level of our performance in life, and can even lead to physical illness, mental fatigue, and emotional depletion. Many people who experience chronic negative stress feel that their lives are out of their control.

That said, rest and relaxation are vital aspects of high performance and happiness. So we have to be careful not to push ourselves too hard without taking time off to rest. This may mean taking a day off from the gym, or a spending the day away from your email inbox.

Time away from the hustle and bustle of daily life is crucial for maintaining a healthy life balance. This life balance minimizes negative stress. By understanding the importance of life balance, our goal of staying out of overwhelm becomes much easier because we can act accordingly. You can't escape a prison that you don't know you're in. Awareness of what causes negative stress is super important for minimizing it.

But how does this relate to quitting the use of porn? Through my personal experience, and numerous self-reports that I've dealt with and analyzed, it has become very apparent that negative stress is a major cause for porn use.

In fact, many men I mentor report that using porn is a way to self-medicate and escape the negative stressors of life. They often feel run down and burnt out from various factors within their life situations, and so they attempt to cope by using porn.

The worst part is that this form of escapism only leads to further negative stress and misery. This habituation pattern leads to a giant negative loop that many men become stuck in. Negative stress, porn, more negative stress and more porn; repeated over and over. This pattern can be extremely tough to get out of.

If this sounds like your situation, I suggest taking out the magnifying glass to take a closer look at your life. What are you unhappy about? Are there any areas that you really need to improve? Are there any specific changes that you should make, but that you've been avoiding?

This might mean having that difficult conversation with a loved one, leaving a job that's draining you, or moving to a new city for a fresh start. Taking an honest look at all aspects of your life will give you a good idea of where you might need to make changes. Awareness of what's triggering this negative loop is the first step toward climbing out of the hole. Then, once you're aware of what you need to do, get down to business and do it. It may be hard, but what's even harder is living life within the negative loop of stress and porn.

If you don't take action to make the necessary changes, the negative loop of stress and porn can lead to medical conditions such as chronic depression and anxiety.

Hypothetically speaking, the porn user, unaware of both the cause of his negative stress and also how porn affects his well-being, feels depressed and anxious, and seeks out a doctor for help. Then the doctor attempts to treat only the symptoms of depression and anxiety, and fails to inquire about this person's life situation, and whether they use internet porn. Then because of the lack of a thorough investigation, these men are misdiagnosed, and put on unnecessary medication. This medication is only a short term solution for their problems. It does well to mask the symptoms, but it doesn't solve the deeper underlying issues that fuel the patient's depression and anxiety. It's like putting a Band-Aid on a wound that needs stitches. This approach doesn't solve anything in the long term.

Much of this can be avoided by simply asking the patient if they are a user of internet porn, and probe deeper into why they choose use it. If they do use porn, have them stop and see what happens to their symptoms of depression and anxiety. Many people experience an evaporation of all symptoms associated with depression and anxiety after extended time off from using internet porn. Then their mind clears up and the cause for their negative stress often becomes apparent. They're finally able to see what's causing their negative stress, and this clearer vision allows them to take the necessary action to make the life changes that are needed.

I understand that this is largely speculative, but I believe that there's potential value in sharing this hypothetical possibility. That said, this may be something to think about if you have both the symptoms of depression and anxiety, and are also a daily user of internet porn.

Regardless, now that we are consciously aware of this negative loop between negative stress and porn, we can design our lives deliberately to achieve a healthy life balance. The proper balance between awareness, action, and attitude can make or break the success of a porn user's recovery.

CHAPTER 8

The Impact of Porn Use | Common Experiences

"Most men lead lives of quiet desperation and go to the grave with the song still in them."

Henry David Thoreau

Below is a list of the most common experiences shared among regular porn users, pulled from online self-reports: (*Your Best Self Now)*

- Low libido
- Porn induced erectile dysfunction
- Development of sexual fetishes inconsistent with sexuality (straight men watching gay porn)
- Depression
- Social anxiety
- Poor social skills
- Brain fog/ lack of mental clarity
- Inability to focus and concentrate

- Inability to remain present to the moment
- Lost enjoyment of past interests
- Desire for isolation
- Desire to escape reality
- Increased vulnerability to addiction
- Increased irritability
- Avoidance of risk
- Increased disagreeableness
- Minimized physical strength
- Minimized physical endurance
- Minimized will power
- Minimized emotional awareness of self
- Minimized emotional awareness of others
- Low motivation
- Lack of life purpose
- Decreased ability to make decisions
- Pessimistic outlook on life

It's important to note that once a porn user quits using and focuses their energy on replacing their porn habit with new healthy, supportive habits, nearly all of these symptoms diminish naturally over time.

So if this list accurately depicts how you feel right now, don't worry. You are on the right path. Just keep reading. With sufficient time and effort, you will heal. And as long as you don't give up on yourself, you can't lose.

CHAPTER 9

Reclaiming Your Power | The Butterfly Effect

"Nothing can bring you peace
but yourself."

Ralph Waldo Emerson

Now that we have established a basis for the importance of understanding the dangers of how porn use affects our life experience, we have to now ask ourselves what we need to do to take our first step toward freedom.

The first step in making any change is awareness, followed by a decision. Once aware of the problem, we must decide that we are willing to implement a solution. In this case, we must decide that we've had enough of feeling empty and helpless. We must decide that our lives are worth making a change. We must decide that we deserve to live life from a space of joy, freedom, and love. And we must decide that we'll do whatever it takes to purify ourselves, and transcend the destructive habit of watching internet pornography.

Our desired change has to become a must. Our recovery depends on our ability to follow through relentlessly on our decision to stop watching porn.

The act of removing porn from our life is an awesome example of one way we can show ourselves self-respect. An interesting phenomena happens when we decide to treat ourselves with increased self-respect, and I call this the Butterfly Effect.

Right now, you're at the beginning of your journey of becoming *A Brand New You*. Right now, you are a caterpillar. You don't have the ability to fly just yet. In order to fly, you have to first enter the cocoon stage. The cocoon stage is where you develop yourself. This is the stage where you consciously treat yourself with unconditional self-respect in a disciplined manner.

As you continue to lead a life of self-respect, you develop within the cocoon. This development takes time, and much of what you are growing within the cocoon won't be completely realized until a little later on. So you keep your faith in yourself and you continue on, treating yourself with self-respect moment by moment, day by day. Eventually you get to the point where you have grown so much that the cocoon can barely hold you any longer.

Then the day finally comes. You squeeze out of your cocoon, and reveal to the world that you have developed the most beautiful set of wings. Colored with the love of the universe, your wings are the most beautiful wings anyone has ever seen. These wings now represent the physical manifestation of your self-love.

It took time, consistency, discipline, and patience, but by treating yourself with unconditional self-respect, you triggered the growth of a colorful, and divine sense of self-love.

By understanding this cause and effect, that from the acts of self-respect grows self-love, it becomes much easier to do things in life that are in alignment with self-respect. You've gained clarity on how to actually love yourself, wholly and fully. This leaves you with an overwhelming sense of joy, and makes evident the value of self-respect.

When you value something, you protect it; you cherish it. This understanding is vital for your success in quitting the use of internet pornography for the long term. And once you fully realize the power of self-respect, all that's left for you to do is to fly on the wings of your manifested self-love, and share your natural beauty with the world.

Once I realized the power that my self-respect has in catalyzing self-love, I gained a new sense of power; a new meaning for life. And as time goes on, my self-love continues to grow, and grow, and grow.

Before you know it, you'll feel that you're floating along on a cloud through life, walking along two inches above the ground, present to the moment, absorbed in abundant joy and effortless wonder. For nothing can do damage to you anymore, because you've reclaimed your power. You've reclaimed your ability to love yourself.

CHAPTER 10

Value, Purpose and Successful Change | Building the House of Your Dreams

---

"Success demands singleness of purpose."

Vince Lombardi

Think of your life during this time of intentional change as being the beginning of building your dream house. You have full control of every acute detail in the design of this house. You can build it in any way that you'd like, with the highest quality materials, and in any location you want. You go on building this house for many months. A ton of time and effort are put into both the planning, and the actual build. Finally, you get to a point where the finishing touches are complete. Your extraordinary house is finally finished.

Do you now go demolish your masterpiece with a crane and bulldozer? Of course not, you value your masterpiece. Since you value the house, you cherish it. You protect it. We must value our lives and our decision to quit using internet pornography in the same way we value building the house of our dreams. We have to protect and cherish this decision if we want change to last. We must be very clear in what we're gaining from sticking to our decision. It also helps to add emotional charge to this decision. The stronger the emotional charge, the stronger the value, and the stronger the value the more purpose you have for sticking to your decision.

It can help to think about how this new lifestyle decision is going to impact your life, your relationships, and how you feel. How is your decision to quit using internet porn going to allow you to become the person who you always knew you could be? What new possibilities is this decision going to bring to your life? What specific value are you gaining?

By being very clear in the value that you'll gain, combined with the linking of that value to a strong emotional charge, and you greatly increase your chance of quitting porn use for good.

The value of this lifestyle change is essentially our higher purpose. This purpose drives us forward at all times during our journey. The strength of this purpose pushes us past the urge to relapse. The power of this purpose propels us forward even in the darkest of nights. When we become lonely, this purpose give us the faith to carry on.

With a strong purpose comes a strong commitment, and from a strong commitment comes discipline, and consistency. And with discipline and consistency, long term lasting change is solidified.

CHAPTER 11

Our Blueprint for Transformation | Harnessing the Power of Habit

---

"We are what we repeatedly do.
Excellence, then, is not an act,
but a habit."

Aristotle

Virtually everything we do from the time we wake up in the morning until the time we go to bed at night, is habit. The power of habit either works in our favor, or works against us. For many of us struggling with quitting an internet porn habit, the power of habit is working against our best interests.

Porn negatively controls how we live our lives, many times without us even realizing it. This below-the-surface negative impact then triggers us to form bad habits in the shape of escapism and self-medication. These bad habits then control our thoughts, beliefs, and behavior.

You be might thinking that you can keep your porn habit, and simply offset it with good habits to negate its negative impact. But I've learned that it's not that simple. Even if we have built our lives on the basis of good habits, if we continue to watch porn, we're blocked from being able to fully experience the benefits of those good habits. The negative impact of porn is too strong, and it keeps us from experiencing the desired growth that motivates us to remain committed to those good habits.

Building a life around healthy habits while continuing to watch porn is like trying to swim a race upstream. You're counterproductive. Your progress is limited due to porn's glass ceiling effect. This one bad habit of watching porn will negatively affect all other areas of your life. Porn use affects your mind, body, spirit, relationships, energy, drive, and enthusiasm. It's like a governor on an engine, regardless of how far you press down the gas, your speed will always be limited.

For example, brain fog and the inability to focus make it difficult to do things that require a clear mind and focused concentration, like reading or meditation. Low motivation and low energy, one of the most commonly reported side effects of porn use, make it difficult to give maximum effort while exercising, which ends up minimizing results. A low libido kills natural attraction and makes it hard to get a date, never mind form a meaningful, romantic relationship. Porn induced erectile dysfunction makes it impossible to have a healthy sex life, and eliminates your ability to utilize sex as a tool to deepen intimacy with your partner. A lack of purpose leads to a lack of fulfillment, and the lack of fulfillment triggers indifference, mediocracy, and hopelessness. Social anxiety makes it difficult to form new friendships which can lead to isolation, and isolation leads to depression. The list goes on and on.

This dynamically negative impact of porn use then causes decreased value associated with each healthy habit. This devaluing of good habits then increases the odds that the porn user will give up on the good altogether. This lack of importance that becomes associated with healthy habits stems directly from the inability to experience the desired positive benefits.

Logically, giving up makes sense. Why work out if you can't put in the necessary effort to make gains? Why read a book if you can't focus well enough to comprehend what you are reading? Why even attempt to date when you can't even get it up? The negative impact of porn use controls a user's life in this way. In their mind, there's no point to even try, because they don't experience any notable change that would motivate them to continue their efforts for improvement.

This creates a giant negative loop that becomes very hard to get out of. By writing off the importance of good habits, it becomes very easy for the porn user to be more and more reliant on porn. Then with increased frequency of use, the porn user risks developing a serious addiction that can lead to more extreme negative side effects, such as chronic depression and even suicidal thoughts.

CHAPTER 12

Becoming the CEO of Your Life | Delegating the Authority of Transformation

---

"Successful people are simply those with successful habits."

Brian Tracy

It's now crystal clear that step one is to delete the porn habit by making the conscious decision to stop watching porn. Then you must focus all of your energy on building your life full of healthy habits that support personal growth.

In a way, you are acting as the CEO of your own life. Great CEOs have the ability to both make decisions quickly and effectively, as well as delegate authority. By removing porn and committing to building a new lifestyle, you're acting decisively. By trusting that the healthy habits will catalyze the desired growth and transformation that you desire, you're essentially delegating the duty of transformation to your healthy habits. By trusting your habits with the authority to transform, all that's left for you to do is remain committed, disciplined, and consistent in your execution of the healthy habits on an everyday basis. Then over time, the desired transformation occurs naturally.

By fully committing to the rebuilding process, we can experience rapid progress that ultimately solidifies into lasting positive change. Our lives only change in direction proportion to our efforts. The measure of the result reflects the measure of the effort. If we really want drastic improvement, we have to give this pursuit our absolute best effort. We've got to decide that positive change is no longer optional. We've got to decide that change MUST happen.

Then we have to raise our standards and commit to meeting them every single day, because we get out of life not what we want, but what we are. If we want more, we have to become more. If we want to improve our lives, we have to first improve ourselves.

The improvement of self also has an added positive affect on the people around us. When people around you witness positive change occurring in your life, they often become motivated to begin their own journey of self-transformation. In this sense, you create a ripple effect of positive change.

As each of us improves, we improve the world. Just imagine how different the world would be if all 7 billion people on this Earth were proactively striving for self-betterment. This outcome is possible, and it starts with you.

CHAPTER 13

Sexual Energy | The Jet Fuel of Self-Transformation

"When driven by his sex energy,
man becomes gifted with a powerful
force for action."

Napoleon Hill

The retaining and preservation of our sexual energy is a vital aspect of the strategy for conquering internet porn use, and achieving lasting self-transformation. Our sexual energy is the most powerful of all human desires. Reproduction is our genes number one priority outside of survival. The need to reproduce has been hard-wired into us over millions of years of evolution, and it arguably controls the majority of how we live our lives.

Imagine what life would look like if we all developed the ability to master and utilize this great force, rather than waste it masturbating to pixels on a screen. Mastering your sexual energy is the x-factor, and the most important aspect of both conquering internet porn addiction, and transforming yourself. The overall idea is to conserve all of your sexual energy, harness it, and then channel it toward fueling your focus of improving other areas of your life. This idea of conserving and repurposing of sexual energy has been around for thousands of years, but has been practiced exclusively in eastern civilizations such as China and India. Somehow, the power of sexual energy has slipped through the cracks of modern society.

I remind you that I'm not an expert on the nuances of these ancient practices. I'm simply a modern day practitioner who has experienced tremendous life changing benefits after trying this out for myself. By adding the element of retaining and transmuting my sexual energy to my lifestyle, I have made profound progress.

I call sexual energy the *Jet Fuel of Self Transformation*, because of how powerfully transformative it is when harnessed and utilized, and how quickly it can transform your life. You're the fighter jet and your sexual energy is the jet fuel, and it's time to take flight.

CHAPTER 14

What to Expect | The "Super Powers"

"Growth is never by mere chance; it is the result of forces working together."

James Cash Penney

The Super Powers. Wow, how captivating. The "super powers" are what first motivated me to remove porn from my life. The time was early in February of 2015, and I had just made the decision to give professional golf a second chance. Four years prior, I had played for one season on a regional mini-tour, but I was forced to put golf on the back burner because of tough times financially. Then, about four years later, my circumstances had improved enough for me to think about giving pro golf another shot, and that's exactly what I did.

I began to research ways to improve myself with the goal of ultimately maximizing my performance of the golf course. I had always been interested in self-mastery and sports psychology, so I began researching all of the ways I could design my life with healthy habits that would result in the improvement of my golfing ability. At the time, I had no intention of ever writing a book on the topic of quitting porn use and self-transformation. I was simply looking for any way to gain an edge on my competition, so I could fulfill my dream of succeeding on the PGA Tour.

During my research on meditation, somehow in the vast landscape of the internet, I came across this idea called "NoFap". This strange word is a term used for abstaining from masturbation and porn use. What caught my attention was the numerous self-reports of men who had adopted this way of life who were claiming to have "super powers."

These men reported feeling like gods. They had increased energy, optimism, confidence, clarity of mind, sharpened focus, deepened concentration, and many more enticing benefits that I will list below. The most amazing part about this discovery was that they all had done just one thing; quit masturbation to high speed internet porn.

At the time, I thought porn and masturbation was "normal" and "healthy". However, I was curious to see whether I would experience these same things in my life if I stopped watching porn and stopped masturbating. I had nothing to lose, so I gave it a shot.

What followed was nothing short of incredible. Once I began stringing together streaks of porn-free living, I began to feel like a god; just like I had read in so many self-reports online! It was absolutely amazing!

What I noticed, was that as my insides changed, so did the world around me. My relationships began to thrive, and I had a new perspective on life. I just felt so damn good that it's hard to put into words. This profound shift in how I felt drove me to continue on, stringing the streaks together.

I felt like I had been granted a second shot at life. I felt like I had been given a chance to redefine myself. Looking back, the experiences that I had in the first few months of abstaining from porn use would mold the direction of the rest of my life. In many ways, quitting porn saved my life. Quitting porn gave me the opportunity to reclaim everything I had felt that I had lost. It was a rebirth for me, and it lit the path for so many amazing changes in my life.

The craziest part of this entire experience was that I had no idea that porn was affecting my life experience in such a negative way. I was clueless. I figured porn use was completely normal, and I had no idea that stopping would eventually change my life so dramatically.

Even though my professional golf career never materialized, my passion for the game still burns brighter than ever. I love to compete, and I will continue to compete for as long as I physically can. Being unsuccessful in professional golf has actually been a blessing in disguise. Had I made it to the PGA Tour, the chances of me writing this book and mentoring others to freedom would have never happened. For that reason, fulfilling my life-long dream of becoming a successful golfer on the PGA Tour was one of the most important things to never happen to me. I am now a vessel for positive change, and I wouldn't change that for anything.

This profound realization of what's possible through living a porn-free lifestyle is what drives me to spread the awareness of the dangers of porn use. Most young people will experience internet porn by the age of 18. Without the proper knowledge, these young people are at an extreme risk to the adverse side effects that manifest after using. The ease of access combined with the elusiveness of the damage that occurs, and many of these young people have little chance of connecting the dots between the negative side effects and their use of porn.

In fact, I have a hunch that people report feeling like they obtain "super powers" once they quit porn because of how accustomed they were to the negative side effects. Once they remove porn use from their lives, they all of a sudden rebound up to a state of natural, healthy well-being. Because this new improved state of being is so profoundly different than their previous state of being, they feel as though they have "super powers".

Below I have compiled a list of my experiences of *The Super Powers*. This is a detailed list of everything that I have experienced within just the first few months of quitting porn, adjusting my attitude, and implementing supportive behaviors that drive a strong sense of healthy well-being.

The Super Powers

- increased overall energy
- increased optimism
- increased self-confidence
- increased self-esteem
- immense self-control
- increased discipline
- increased risk tolerance
- increased women attraction (strong eye contact)
- increased acknowledgement from men and strangers
- increased kindness
- increased self-awareness
- boosted creativity
- improved memory
- evaporation of social anxiety
- increased desire to be social
- increased libido
- sharper mental clarity
- sharper focus and concentration
- increased motivation
- increased physical strength
- higher pain tolerance
- overall sense of heightened well-being

CHAPTER 15

A Sign of Progress | The Infamous Wet Dream

"You don't make progress by standing on the sidelines, whimpering and complaining. You make progress by implementing ideas."

Shirley Chisholm

Inevitably, when we retain our sexual energy by refraining from any sort of sexual release for an extended period of time, there comes a point where your body must release, regardless of conscious choice. This most commonly known as a wet dream. You basically wake up, without warning, to a mess in your pants. Unpleasant, yes. But wet dreams are a natural part of life and nothing to be ashamed of. Wet dreams are most common in adolescence, but once a male becomes regularly sexual active, wet dreams usually cease.

In fact, I had never experienced a wet dream until the age of 25, when I began preserving my sexual energy in pursuit of quitting porn. I was regularly sexually active from the age of 14 onward, so my body had no reason to release involuntarily during my sleep. I never built up enough sexual energy to trigger the need for an involuntary release.

If you're like me, and have never had any past experience with wet dreams, they can completely blindside you and leave you confused, curious, and even disappointed when you experience one unexpectedly. Once you give up porn and begin to preserve your sexual energy, it's almost guaranteed that you'll experience one at one point or another. It's important to be aware of this so you don't become discouraged.

Many men wake up to this mess, puzzled as to what the heck happened, and why. The first thing that comes to their mind is "does this count as a relapse?" The answer to that question is no. Wet dreams don't count as a relapse. I suggest that a wet dream is simply a sign that your body is in the process of adjusting to your new lifestyle of preserving your sexual energy.

This can be compared to your strength when you first begin lifting weights. Starting out, you're weak and can only lift a certain amount of weight. However, as time passes and you continue to lift, you eventually increase your strength, which allows you to lift heavier weights.

Your body works in this same way when retaining sexual energy. At first, your body may not be able to handle that much energy, and you might have a wet dream after just 3 or 4 days of retaining. However, with time your body will adjust, and your ability to retain increases. Then you might find that you can go 30 days without a wet dream, where as in the beginning you could only go 3 or 4 days.

As time passes, wet dreams become less frequent. So rather than being discouraged by them, treat wet dreams as a barometer of your personal progress. View wet dreams as a sign that good changes are happening within you. View wet dreams as a testament to your mental strength, self-discipline, and commitment to not give in to your sexual urges. Because when you give in to your sexual urges and release regularly, wet dreams simply don't happen.

From this perspective, wet dreams are simply a sign that you are actively making progress. I remember feeling like I had lost all of my progress after my first wet dream because I didn't understand why it had happened. I put myself through unnecessary suffering because I felt like I had relapsed. It wasn't until I realized that I would continue to have wet dreams every 2-3 months as long as I retained my sexual energy that I was able to understand they are just a part of the process.

It became apparent to me over time that wet dreams are just the body's way of intermittently releasing when necessary, and that they become less frequent the longer you live this lifestyle. Take my word for it, and avoid unnecessary discouragement.

CHAPTER 16

But Can I Have Sex? | Preserving the Rebooting & Rewiring of Your Brain

"He who would accomplish little must sacrifice little; he who would achieve much must sacrifice much; he who would attain highly must sacrifice greatly."

James Allen

"I've decided to quit pornography and I understand the concept of retaining my sexual energy for sexual transmutation, but can I still have sex?"

By far this is the most frequently asked question by individuals whom I mentor. They want to successfully quit using porn, but they also want to know if they can have sex in the process. My best advice is that for anyone with a serious porn addiction, refraining from sex for the time that it takes to quit porn for good is a must.

So no, until you know with every ounce of your being that you have gotten over your porn habit, you should refrain from any type of sexual activity. This time period is different for everyone, but I recommend at least 60 days without any sexual activity. For people with more extreme addictions, this reboot can take multiple months.

The reasoning for refraining from sex during reboot is to avoid relapse, and to allow your brain enough time to heal. I'll avoid butchering the science behind what happens within your brain during and after watching porn by just saying that this whole process takes time. And as you take time away from using porn, the negative effects will be reversed naturally.

When you do eventually reboot, at that point it will be safe to develop a new relationship with sex (Chapter 36). The time is takes to fully reboot varies between individuals and depends on the severity of their addiction, and the length of time that they have been addicted. Age also seems to be a factor. Young men who have grown up watching porn often take more time to reboot than older men who adopted their porn habit later in life.

For me, I reached the point where I knew in my heart that I was done with porn after about two months into my attempt at quitting. This two month span was the time it took to battle through relapses, and put together 30 days in a row of porn-free living. After putting together that 30 day streak, I knew that there was no way I would ever go back. The benefits were just too good. It was at this point that I knew it was safe for me to have sex if the opportunity arose, without risking relapsing later once the sex wasn't available.

The reboot process requires a great deal of time, patience, and discipline. But it's well worth it. Nothing worth having comes easy. When you reach the point where you know in your heart that this is the lifestyle you're going to live for the long term, only then will you know what it feels like to be truly free. This realization marks the first taste of liberation. As you continue on, the wonder and joys of life will continue to manifest more deeply, and you'll know in your heart that there is no way you'll ever go back to using porn.

CHAPTER 17

What about my Wife? | The Importance of Communication

"If you just communicate, you can get by. But if you communicate skillfully, you can work miracles."

Jim Rohn

This section is dedicated to anyone who is in a relationship. A disturbing fact is that more than half of divorces list pornography use as one of the main contributing factors for the demise of the relationship. This means if you're in a relationship or married, and you are a regular porn user, your relationship is at a much higher risk of failure.

You can avoid ruining your relationship by understanding the risks and consequences of porn use, and then by taking appropriate action. The appropriate action is very simple; quit using porn!

So let's say you're in agreement, and you've decided to quit. That's the easy part. The hard part is that you're now faced with the decision to either tell your wife or girlfriend, or keep it a secret. I hope that your relationship has a strong enough foundation of trust that you can disclose anything to your partner. Trust and communication are vital aspects of a successful relationship. If you have complete trust in one another, and have the ability to communicate effectively, you are much more likely to succeed in the long term. It's only when you lack in either of these categories that you have a much higher chance of relationship failure, and I believe that trust and communication go hand in hand. When you fully trust someone, your lines of communication are completely open, because you don't fear how they may react.

However, even when you have complete trust in someone, sharing the fact that you have an internet porn problem is still very difficult. If you lack trust in your partner, you'll without a doubt keep your porn problem a secret. However, hiding your porn problem only makes your journey to liberation much more challenging, as well as risking the success of your intimate relationship altogether.

I learned the importance of trust and communication the hard way from first-hand experience. My father and mother separated in 2016, and their main issue was a lack of communication. No, porn wasn't the problem, but effective communication was. They had been married for 26 years before their separation. As old as I was at the time, this separation was still hard on me. However, I did learn the profound value of communication and trust that's required to make a relationship fruitful, fulfilling, and successful over the long term.

Given the toxicity of my parents living together in the same house, the separation was necessary. The resistance that you could feel when they were in the same room was extremely uncomfortable. This resistance was a product of the resentment that had manifested from a lack of communication and trust over many years. This resentment bled into every other area of their relationship, and ultimately the damage done was beyond repair. Separation was the only option. Don't allow this same situation to play out in your life, and save yourself the heart ache by being proactive.

You can learn from this unfortunate outcome just as I have, without having to actually go through the pain of a break up, by acting right now. If you can feel the hesitation associated with sharing your porn problem with your partner, don't wait any longer; act now. The longer you think about it, the harder it will be to talk about. Take responsibility for yourself. Honesty is indispensable. What might feel very awkward and uncomfortable at first, will pay off big time in the long run.

You also shouldn't be ashamed of having a porn problem because of how addicting porn is. It's not your fault. Many porn users are completely unaware of how porn affects the mind, body, and spirit, and how it in turn will affect every area of your life. Made aware of the negative impact, and many porn users jump on removing the habit from their lives immediately. It's only your fault when you understand the magnitude of the consequences of porn use, and continue to use it anyway.

Sharing your internet porn use problem with your partner may be the single most difficult obstacle that you come across on this entire journey. But by completely opening up to your partner, there is a high chance that you'll actually grow closer. Numerous men whom I have given this advice to have reported that this level of openness has deepened their connection exponentially. These same men have also reported a much easier road to recovery because they no longer felt alone. Loneliness can be paralyzing. By having someone in your corner fighting for you every step of the way, your journey to full recovery will be much easier.

Although it may seem very difficult to disclose this part of you, it's very crucial in the preservation of your intimate relationship, as well as your ultimate recovery from porn use. So take the plunge, and say what's hard to say. You'll thank yourself later. You may even look back at this entire porn use issue, and see it as a blessing. You may see it as a catalyst for a deeper, more meaningful connection with your partner.

What you go through, grows you. Open up your lines of communication and don't hold back. Do what is hard. If you do what is hard, your life will be easy. If you do what is easy, your life will be hard. Go ahead and act in the name of love, act in the name of devotion, and act in the name of commitment. Open yourself completely, and never look back.

CHAPTER 18

Our Treasure Map | Three Major Checkpoints of Our Journey

"The journey of a thousand miles starts with a single step."

Lao Tzu

There's three major checkpoints that we all pass through as we evolve on this journey of quitting porn. These checkpoints define definite stages of growth, and being aware of them will help you navigate your way. Each of these checkpoints are of equal importance.

The first checkpoint is the *"inspired"* stage. This is the stage where you become inspired to make a decision to change your life. This is the stage where you become aware of how your use of internet porn is negatively affecting your life. This is the stage where you take a stand and hold your ground. This is the stage where you shine your light of consciousness on the destruction this habit has caused you, and decide that enough is enough. This is the stage where you decide to carve a new path through life; a path that is filled with joy, content, and freedom. This checkpoint is essentially a promise to yourself that commits yourself indefinitely to moving towards becoming the best you that you can possibly be.

The second checkpoint is the *"transformation"* stage. This is the stage after you have made your decision to quit using porn, but before you know in your heart that you have conquered it. This is the stage where you take massive action. This is the battle stage. This is the stage where you slay the dragon, by building a completely new lifestyle. This stage is best described by Socrates' quote, "The secret of change is to focus all of your energy, not in fighting the old, but in building the new." This is the stage where you rebuild your life style. This is the stage where you fight and win the war. This is the stage where you remove one bad habit from your life, and replace it with many positive, supportive habits. These habits will propel you forward, and allow you to ride on the wings of the universe straight into a state of presence, ease, satisfaction, and freedom. This is the stage where you transform yourself.

The third checkpoint is the *"evolve"* stage. During this stage, you're simply continuing to build upon your healthy habits, and remain committed to your lifestyle. The difference though, is that you're in a place where the construction is done, and you must simply maintain. This stage is the stage where you know deep within yourself that no matter what happens in life, there's no going back to your old lifestyle of watching internet porn.

When you find yourself in this stage, you'll have transcended your porn use habit. You'll find yourself proud of the person you've become, and proud of the life you've built. You'll find yourself content with life, but eager for what is to come. You'll find yourself grateful for all of your growth, and even more grateful for your life.

Life takes on a new meaning in the third stage. Getting to a place where you know in your heart that you have transcended the terrible porn habit is an amazing place to be. Language is clumsy in the attempt to accurately describe what it feels like. If I had only two words to describe the feeling of this transcendence, those two words are love and freedom.

PART II: The Action to Transform

"Action is the foundational key to all success."

Pablo Piccaso

CHAPTER 19

The 11 Pillars of Change | Introduction

"The secret of change is to focus all of your energy, not on fighting the old, but on building the new."

Socrates

It's time to shift our focus away from quitting porn, and instead focus our energy on the rebuilding process. We must now focus on adding healthy, productive habits into our lives. These positive habits keep us feeling great, and feeling great gives us the best chance to avoid reverting back to our old lifestyle of watching internet pornography.

By stacking habits that have similar positive effects on our mind, body and spirit energies, we create a solid foundation for long-term self-transformation. These powerful transformative habits are called *The 11 Pillars of Change*. By implementing *The 11 Pillars of Change* into our lives, we create extreme positive momentum that carries us far away from the use of internet porn, and expedites our self-transformation. Combined with feeling much better, the fact that you're busy participating proactively in the development of yourself gives you very little time to even think about going back to using internet porn.

I've lived this strategy for years, and have used it with hundreds of young men whom I've mentored with great success. Even still, relapses happen. They're just a part of the process. However, having an action system in place where you know what you have to do regardless of whether you relapse, is extremely vital for achieving lasting change. Relapses can feel devastating, but when there's a healthy habit system already in place, a relapse becomes a minor speed bump. By knowing what you must do to continue progress in the wake of a relapse is key to being able to get back on track and prevent further stagnation.

However, if you don't have a healthy habit system in place, or do not understand the strategy behind this habit-based action plan, you'll easily slide right back down the dark rabbit hole of porn and masturbation. By having a system in place, you can simply climb back on the horse and continue on your journey, because you know exactly what you need to do to pick up where you left off.

The 11 Pillars of Change focus on actively taking care of our mind, body and spirit. By taking proper action to build up each of these areas, we set ourselves up for success in becoming the strongest versions of ourselves and achieving long-term healthy well-being. Health and well-being is not something we invented. Health and well-being is simply life happening free from negativity, in a state of ease and flow.

When we fully commit to adopting this lifestyle, we see rapid improvements in our energy levels, motivation, zest for life, and how we feel about ourselves. Below I have listed *The 11 Pillars of Change* that our rebuilding process is centered on. We'll explore these in extensive depth in the coming pages.

- The 1st Pillar of Change | Exercise | Effective Stress Management
- The 2nd Pillar of Change | Meditation | Deliberately Doing Nothing
- The 3rd Pillar of Change | Journaling | Self-Talk Mastery & Character Development
- The 4th Pillar of Change | Super-Socialization | Cultivating a Sense of Belonging
- The 5th Pillar of Change | Social Media DETOX | Dropping Comparison and Judgement
- The 6th Pillar of Change | Passion Pursuits | Eliminating Boredom
- The 7th Pillar of Change | Motivational Material | Powering through the Dreaded Flatline
- The 8th Pillar of Change | Relapse Remedies | The Power of Shifted Focus
- The 9th Pillar of Change | Cold Shower Therapy | Compounded Will-Power

- The 10th Pillar of Change | Floatation Therapy | Floating to Freedom
- The 11th Pillar of Change | Rituals | Two Routines for Routine Growth

The 11 Pillars of Change are our primary focus in terms of what action we must take to give ourselves the best chance for a full long-term recovery from internet porn use. Committing to carrying out these activities on a daily basis sets us up for growth well beyond porn addiction. Over time, you'll become a new person. You'll crush barriers, and leap past perceived limits at an astounding pace.

Humans are growth driven beings. In order to be fulfilled in life, we have to cultivate and maintain a strong sense of personal growth. By carrying out these activities on a regular basis, we successfully nurture this sense of growth. We're then fueled by our progress, and this propels us forward.

The empowerment of taking control of your life and experiencing real results is a priceless feeling. There are no limits to the growth we can make when we stay dedicated to the process, and remain disciplined in moving forward every single day. *The 11 Pillars of Change* are the core habits that promote this profound sense of growth, that wouldn't otherwise be experienced.

CHAPTER 20

The 1st Pillar of Change | Exercise | Effective Stress Management

---

"Training gives us an outlet for suppressed energies created by stress and thus tones the spirit just as exercise conditions the body."

Arnold Schwarzenegger

The 1st Pillar of Change is daily exercise. Daily exercise is paramount for success in both quitting porn and self-transformation. Daily exercise multiplies our built up sexual energy, relieves stress, and strengthens our mind-body-spirit connection. Exercise also grows our ability to deal with uncomfortable situations by getting us accustomed to pain during our work outs. Through dealing with physical pain we become not only physically stronger, but mentally and spiritually stronger.

This mental toughness plays a huge role not only in our efforts of getting over porn, but in dealing with the challenges of life in general. With consistent physical training, we begin to see our self as someone who can take on challenges and succeed in overcoming them. You begin to see yourself as a warrior of life. You begin to relish the difficulties of life because you see yourself as someone who wins. You see yourself as someone who's strong and resilient. This new vision of yourself then transfers to every other area of your life. You begin to confront things that you might've been avoiding. You begin to step boldly into uncertainty with confidence, and you push back against the resistances of life.

Daily exercise also multiplies your energy. Most people think that if they work out all the time, that they'll get tired. In fact, the exact opposite is what occurs. By working out consistently, you gain energy rather than lose it. You then ride this wave of increased energy throughout your day. This increased energy helps you be more productive, effective and efficient in your daily activities.

Then, as you realize how much more you're able to accomplish because of your increased energy levels, you naturally place added importance on your workouts. The added importance of exercise then shifts your perception of working out from a chore, to an activity that makes your life experience better.

Once your perception shifts and you understand the huge value exercise brings to your life, your workouts then become something you look forward to. You no longer have to muster up the motivation to work out, and you gain massive forward momentum.

Exercise is also a vital habit to add to your lifestyle when you are quitting porn, because it makes you feel marvelous! And when you feel marvelous, staying away from using porn is a piece of cake.

Along with feeling awesome, training everyday also triggers a physical transformation. As you become physically stronger and your endurance improves, your body begins to change. This physical transformation adds to the fire. Your motivation spikes, and pushing yourself becomes a lot of fun. Your physical transformation has a positive impact on your self-confidence, self-image, and self-esteem. This positive feedback encourages you to keep plowing ahead in order to keep seeing results.

The added motivation to keep pushing forward fast tracks your transformation. It keeps you committed and disciplined even when you don't really feel like working out. It's this strong sense of discipline and commitment that solidifies positive change. For all of these reasons, anyone who wants to transform well beyond quitting porn has to commit themselves to daily physical exercise. Everyday execution is crucial for supporting a dynamic, life-changing transformation of self.

CHAPTER 21

The 2nd Pillar of Change | Meditation | Deliberately Doing Nothing

---

"Meditation is an opportunity to move into a dimension where there is no such thing as stress within you."

Sadhguru

The 2nd Pillar of Change is daily meditation. Meditation is a paramount core habit for both quitting porn permanently and fast tracking self-growth. You've probably heard of it, but you might be wondering what meditation is. The simplest answer to that question is that meditation is the act of deliberately doing nothing. Meditation requires that you take the time, often just 10 or 15 minutes, to sit down comfortably with your eyes closed, and do absolutely nothing.

Purposely doing nothing allows you to quiet the mind, and allows you to disconnect from the hustle and bustle of everyday life. In a world with constant hyper-stimulation, meditation is more valuable than ever before. Unplugging from the world greatly increases our ability to function at a high level once we choose to get back to our daily activities.

Think of yourself as a cell phone. In order for a cell phone to function in the best way that it possibly can, it needs to be charged on a regular basis. Humans are no different. By taking time every single day to sit down and meditate, we're essentially charging ourselves. By consistently charging ourselves, we maximize our ability to perform our absolute best when we get back into the arena of everyday life.

However, there's some negative stigma surrounding meditation. Some people are skeptical to try it because it's associated with certain religions. Some people also dismiss it before understanding how it works. I've learned that the best way to approach meditation is with a beginner's mind. If you're someone who has written off meditation as being useless, please wipe the slate clean, and do your best to approach this concept with an open mind.

I'm not identified with any religion. I'm probably one of the least knowledgeable people on Earth when it comes to theology. When someone asks me my religion, my answer is love. Love governs my actions. I'm a practitioner, and I only do things that make my life experience better, and meditation is one of those things.

I've used meditation to maximize my well-being for many years. I started meditating on a daily basis because I thought that it would improve my ability to focus, concentrate, and give me clarity of mind, which would then translate to lower golf scores. In high school, I used hypnosis for these same reasons, and I experienced phenomenal results.

I'll briefly touch on these performances to give you an idea of the power of the mind when it's clear, focused, and positive. I share my success in competitive golf not to boast, but to show how an efficient mind can translate into superior results.

I'm not physically gifted. I'm barely 5'5", and during my adolescent years I weighed 125 pounds soaking wet. My physical ability wasn't the reason for my success. I attribute my success as an amateur golfer in tournament play to my mental toughness, which allowed me to consistently separate myself from my competition. However, during the height of my porn use, my golf performances reflected my presiding condition of my mind. My porn use weakened my mental strength. This weakening had a tremendously negative impact on my competitive performances.

These poor performances then dimmed my fire for competitive golf, and eventually lead me to a four year period where I barely played at all. However, I revived my competitive fire once I quit using porn. It was restored naturally. I'll briefly describe my pre-porn golf career to paint a better picture of the power of a clear, focused, strong, and efficient mind.

I won my first Club Championship at the age of 14 at Tekoa Country Club. I also won back to back Men's Club Championships at the Ranch Golf Club, as well as 4 straight Junior Club Championships. I tied for 1st in the 2005 MA State High School Championship, and placed 2nd in the 2006 New England High School Championship. I earned First-Team All-Region all four years of high school, and finished my senior year ranked #1 in scoring average for my respective region.

I attribute most of my achievements as a junior golfer to my daily hypnosis sessions with my grandmother. I began being hypnotized by my grandmother when I was 14 years old. These hypnosis sessions were very similar to the daily meditation I practice currently. I would lay down, close my eyes, and focus on becoming very relaxed. Then my grandmother would read positive statements related to golf and high performance. These hypnosis sessions lasted no longer than 15 minutes, but they were crucial for maximizing my performance. Bobby Jones once said that "Golf is a game played on a five-inch course- the space between your ears." I'm confident that my mental toughness cultivated through regular hypnosis was the x-factor for my early success in golf.

My success in golf continued into college. During my two-year tenure at Holyoke Community College, I won 12 tournaments including back to back Region 21 titles. In 2008 I earned First-Team All-American honors for the first time in school history. I played my junior and senior seasons at American International College, where I won twice.

I turned pro after college in 2011. This was the same time period where my porn use began to escalate into an everyday habit. In hindsight, my mindset and attitude towards life reflected this fact, as well as my performance on the golf course. I wasn't performing as well as I knew that I could, and my motivation to compete eventually completely died out. After just one season, I put the clubs away to go to work full-time, and surrendered my dream to the idea of mediocracy.

Looking back it's easy to see that my surrender was greatly influenced by my porn habit. This coincided with a difficult financial situation that my family was going through at the time. It was the perfect storm. I encountered a difficult, pressure packed situation, and at the same time was draining my life force energy by using porn. I was then unable to deal with the situation in a healthy manner. Instead, I spiraled down the dark rabbit hole of porn use in an attempt to numb the pain of the reality of my life situation.

Four years later, I decided to make a second effort at professional golf. This was when I began researching meditation, as well as other ways that I could maximize my ability to perform on the golf course. At the time, I had no intention of ever becoming a "spiritual person". I simply wanted to give myself the best chance that I could at performing at a high level, just like I did growing up.

About a month passed of daily meditation, and I began to notice significant positive changes in how I perceived life, as well as how I felt. These changes continued to grow, and my meditation practice would end up being a key factor in shaping the direction of my life from there on out. During this same time of committing myself to daily meditation, I gave up watching porn. This combination of no porn and meditation was life changing.

I began to notice how mindfulness was bleeding into my everyday life. My golf scores didn't improve right away, but my thoughts, mood, and feelings sure did. I gained the ability to effortlessly maintain a higher mood, and an optimistic mindset. It felt so natural. I also realized that literally nothing bothered me anymore. I became less triggered by events, people, or situations that in the past would have caused me to lose my cool.

My patience continued to increased, and my mind became clear. My emotional awareness for both myself and others began to deepen as well. I became keenly aware of how my actions influenced how I felt. Therefore, I began to control my feelings by controlling my behavior. My focus and concentration also became stronger, and I began performing daily work tasks with increased effectiveness and efficiency. Tedious tasks actually became enjoyable. These improvements were a lot of fun to experience.

The changes I've experienced since meditating on a daily basis have been nothing short of amazing. Meditation has been a vital tool for transforming myself into the changed man that I am today. Daily practice has helped me to feel awesome regardless of the external circumstances of my life. It's made me immune to the negativity that once plagued my life, and has helped me to live every moment to the best of my ability from a place of unconditional love for myself, others, and the world.

By feeling great on a consistent basis, giving up the use of porn became very easy. There's no doubt in my mind that meditation played a very important role in my dramatic transformation. The best thing is that everyone can tap into these benefits by meditating for just 10 minutes a day. That's right, you don't have to become a monk to reap the rewards of meditation!

Below I have comprised simplified lists of the physical, mental, and spiritual benefits that I've experienced from daily meditation practice.

The Physical Benefits of Meditation:

- Exponential self-healing (I have Crohn's disease, and have been in remission since committing to daily practice)
- Decreased tension-related pain
- Improved mood
- Decreased reactivity to the external factors of life
- Increased energy levels

The Mental & Spiritual Benefits of Meditation:

- Increased happiness
- Increased compassion
- Increased non-judgement of self, and others
- Increased creativity
- Increased ability to relax
- Increased clarity of mind
- Increased ability to focus and concentrate
- Increased awareness of intuition
- Decreased anxiety
- Decreased attachment to negative thoughts and emotions

But How Do I Meditate?

I know what you're thinking, it all sounds great, but how do I do it? How do I meditate?

While I am not an expert on teaching meditation, I do have insights that I've gained in my many years of practice. I have hundreds of hours invested in my own meditation practice. These hours are logged on an app on my cell phone. That said, my first piece of advice for motivated meditators is to invest in a meditation app on your smartphone. There are a growing number of apps to choose from, and these apps are absolutely awesome for beginners. By utilizing an app, you can learn how to meditate step by step with the guidance of experts in the field.

My favorite app for meditation is *Calm*. *Calm* is an incredible app that has a variety of themed meditations, sleep stories, mindfulness programs, as well as a daily meditation called the *Daily Calm*. They have specific programs designed for happiness, gratitude, self-esteem, forgiveness, breaking bad habits, and so much more.

The creators of *Calm* are always updating and improving their app, which keeps things fresh and interesting. The majority of their guided meditations range from 2 minutes to 20 minutes. This gives you the power to have complete control over how long you choose to sit. *Calm* also offers unguided meditation sessions that give you the ability to customize your session length.

Calm combines insightful guidance with relaxing background sounds of the user's choice. A user can choose background sounds from settings such as a mountain lake, fireplace, sunset beach, summer meadow, Zen Ocean, and many more. The ability to customize the details of the user's experience is what has kept me using *Calm* for so long. There's always something that can be tweaked to keep the practice fresh.

In my opinion, the variety and flexibility that *Calm* offers makes it the most efficient, effective and most user-friendly app to use for daily meditation. However, the full version of *Calm* isn't free. The full version costs $60 per year, which is a cheap price to pay for the benefits that it offers. That said, *Calm* does offer a 7 day mindfulness program that's free to try out. This way you can experiment and find out if their app suits your needs.

I've been a paying customer for over three years, and I have no plan to change that. *Calm* has made me a customer for life. Try it out for yourself, and see how you like it. *Calm* has made daily meditation easy, enjoyable and something I look forward to every day. If you come to find that *Calm* doesn't fit your needs, there's a plethora of other meditation apps on the market that you could try.

No smartphone? No problem.

If you don't have access to a smartphone, or can't utilize an app like *Calm*, all hope isn't lost. You can still meditate.

The concept of meditation has been around for thousands of years before smart phone technology was ever invented.

Let's do a quick rundown of how you can meditate without using a smartphone app. My first piece of advice is to start by blocking off 10 minutes of your day, every day, to sit someplace where there are no distractions. The morning is a great time to meditate, because it helps you to start the day with a fresh mind. However, there is value in evening meditations as well. Meditating in the evening can help you to disconnect and relax after a long day. Everyone is different, so experiment and see what works best for you and your lifestyle.

You can choose anyplace to meditate. This might mean sitting in your living room, back porch, or even on a blanket at your local park. Once you find your location, sit comfortably with your eyes closed, and focus on FEELING your breath. Everyone feels their breath differently; some feel it in their chest, some their nose, and some their lips. It doesn't matter where you choose to focus, what's important is that you gently rest that focus on the inhales and exhales for an extended period of time.

Ten minutes of practice per day is sufficient. This type of meditation is called noting. There are other types of meditation, such as body scans, but I've found that this style of noting is the best for beginners because of its simplicity.

Also, don't worry about the repetitive nature of your thoughts. Thoughts happen. When you notice your mind wandering, just simply acknowledge this, and kindly bring your focus back to your breathe.

At first, you'll notice that you'll have to refocus your attention quite often. Don't worry. This is completely normal. That's why it's called meditation "practice". As you continue to practice, you will become better and better at quieting the mind, and creating space between you and your thoughts. Meditation is like anything else, it takes time and practice to improve. With consistent disciplined practice, major benefits will be experienced.

One of the keys to tapping into the powerful benefits of meditation is to practice every single day. Don't skip any day. Consistent daily practice then becomes a habit, and over time you'll begin to notice how your growing state of presence bleeds over into other areas of your life.

It's also important to note that it won't take long to experience benefits. It took me about a month of every day practice before I began to notice changes in how I felt, and how I perceived life. This is important because as you feel better and better, you'll be less inclined to go back to using porn.

CHAPTER 22

The 3rd Pillar of Change | Journaling | Self-Talk Mastery & Character Development

"I can shake off everything as I write;
my sorrows disappear,
my courage is reborn."

Anne Frank

The 3rd Pillar of Change is journaling. In life, you can either choose to be your own biggest fan, or your own worst critic. For many of us, becoming our own biggest fan is quite the challenge. To do so successfully means that we have to learn to master our self-talk.

We are literally the creators of ourselves, and regardless of whether we like it or not, our self-talk is the main factor in our creation. Self-talk impacts our beliefs, and our beliefs impact our thoughts. Then our thoughts impact our behavior, and our behavior solidifies into habit. Habit then molds the circumstances of our lives.

That said, we have two choices that we can make. We can either take control of the creation of ourselves, or we can remain complacent, and be at the mercy of the external world in terms of what we believe. There's also no stopping this creative process. With that in mind, I suggest that we take responsibility for how we think about ourselves, rather than remain complacent. By taking full responsibility and mastering our self-talk, we then create by choice, rather than by default.

Think of yourself as a super-computer, and your self-talk is the software that allows it to operate. Poor quality software makes for a poorly operating computer, whose capabilities are severely limited. On the other hand, if you use high quality software, this computer not only runs well, but it thrives.

Our life experience works in this same way. Our self-talk plays a major role in determining the quality of our life experience. But what is our self-talk comprised of? Our self-talk is comprised of the thoughts that we choose to focus on, and the stories we tell ourselves. By learning to focus on positive thoughts, and stories that empower us, we afford ourselves the highest probability of making our life experience the best that we possibly can.

The best way to master our self-talk is to write in a journal every single day. Below are the benefits that I've experienced since committing to regular journaling practice.

The Benefits of Writing in a Journal:

- Efficiently process negative emotions
- Reinforce and savor positive emotions
- Reflect, analyze, and program desired thoughts and behaviors
- Help to catalyze the embodiment of positive affirmations which aids character development
- Helpful to reframe negative outcomes with gratitude for what can be learned
- Helpful to catalyze feelings of non-judgement, non-attachment, and acceptance
- Deepens and strengthens your connection with your intuition

Writing is the gateway to the subconscious mind. And we all know that the subconscious mind is infinitely more powerful than our conscious mind. That said, writing in a journal is one of the greatest tools we can use to achieve inner peace, and develop the desired character traits of our ideal self.

Once you begin to write on a regular basis, you notice a feeling of serenity within yourself. There's a distinct difference in how I feel if I skip even just one writing session. Feeling this sense of jumbled-ness after skipping a session really puts into perspective how important a tool journaling is for maintaining a strong sense of well-being. The relief felt after writing becomes a major motivator, and will give you a powerful reason to stay committed to writing every day.

One of the coolest things that I've learned is that there's no wrong way to write in a journal. The most important thing is that you remain consistent and dedicated to daily practice. Consistency and discipline is what drives desired results.

The journaling.strategy that works best for me, is writing in the morning as soon as I wake up, and writing and at night right before I go to bed. Each of these sessions take about 10 minutes each, and I fill up one side of a white lined piece of paper. I use a standard one subject notebook that you can buy at Walmart for less than a dollar.

Writing in the morning helps to start the day on a positive note, and helps to build forward momentum. How you begin each day has a huge impact on how the rest of your day goes. If you can win the morning, you can win the day.

My evening writing session helps me to gain closure for the day, process negative emotions, and reflect on how I feel about what ever events are happening in my life. By writing consistently, I'm able to analyze my lifestyle, and zero in on what may or may not be working. Then, I can adjust my life style accordingly.

Journaling Technique #1 | Free Writes

There are two primary journaling techniques that I use on an everyday basis that are both simple and effective for self-talk mastery and character development. The first style I use is called a free write. A free write is when you jot down all of your thoughts and allow yourself to vent, reflect, reframe, or write about whatever your heart feels is necessary. This style of writing always gives me a good sense of closure regarding my thoughts, feelings and actions.

My bedtime journal session is usually a free write. However, I follow no specific rules. Sometimes I'll go multiple days between free writes. I follow my heart in terms of what I feel is necessary for each specific session. There are other times when I'll do three or four free writes in a row. It all depends on what's going on in my life at that particular time.

Example Free-Write Journal Entry:

"Thank you for my health and my healing. I am so blessed to be on this path of self-purification. I can feel the many differences that living this lifestyle is making in both how I feel and how I perceive life. I can feel my confidence growing. I can feel my social anxiety evaporating. I feel like a brand new person. People are treating me differently and I am getting so many more smiles wherever I go. I never knew that giving up my porn habit would have this many benefits. I am excited for

further growth and development. I am eager to take on more responsibility at work and it feels great to be free from negativity. I am so grateful for my life and the amazing group of people who love and support me unconditionally. It feels amazing to be able to feel again. It feels amazing to have a clear mind. I am so thankful that I have come this way. Life will never be the same. I choose love. I send love. I receive love. I am love."

Journaling Technique #2 | Positive Affirmations

The second journaling technique that I use is positive affirmations. The main goal of positive affirmations is to first specify my desired character traits that I want to embody, and then to focus on them. These desired character traits are the character traits of my ideal self. Listing positive affirmations is my main technique for character development. This technique uses list format, in the present tense.

Once again, I have no rules for which technique I choose to utilize for each particular session. I operate completely on feel. However, the trend is that most of my positive affirmation entries are written during my morning journaling session.

My typical routine is to list out all of the character traits that I want to embody in the present tense. My goal is to fill up an entire page in a one subject notebook. Once I fill the page, I circle back and use a highlighter to highlight each character trait, as I reread the list. This helps to reinforce each affirmation, and also adds some color to my journal. Highlighting my entries have become something that I really enjoy doing. After I finish re-reading and highlighting, I close my journal and go about my day.

Writing positive affirmations every day over a long period of time programs your subconscious mind, and allows you to take full control of your character development. At first, writing affirmations may seem cheesy. But as time passes, you'll find that you begin to naturally embody the character traits that you choose to focus on.

You literally create yourself, entry by entry. Looking back at my past self, before I started writing every day, and it's clear to see that I was at the complete mercy of the external world in terms of who I was as a person. After years of writing, I now know that I am the maker of myself. I now know that I hold the key to transformation, and that key is a pen.

My relentlessly consistent journaling practice has made me a more resilient and virtuous person. I'm unshakable. The inner peace that I've developed is priceless. I am a big heap of clay, and the very words I write mold the clay into a sculpture representing my ideal self. They say "fake it until you make it", but I fake it until I become it.

The X-Factor for Embodiment | FEELING

A crucial tip for maximizing the effectiveness of positive affirmations, is to FEEL deeply into them. The deeper I feel into each trait, the more effective I show up in the world as an expression of each specific trait. The feeling aspect of positive affirmations is the bridge between thinking and becoming.

Feeling creates embodiment. In order to embody a trait, it's important to link the specific positive affirmation with a specific a memory that's congruent to that specific trait.

For example, for the affirmation *I am confident*, I would think about a time in the past where I acted with high confidence. This could be a time when I aced a presentation in college, won a golf tournament, or when I asked a pretty girl on a date.

The example that you link to the affirmation is irrelevant. The most important thing is that the link stirs up a positive, powerful feeling that's congruent with that specific character trait. The more powerful the feeling, the quicker and easier you will embody that particular trait. Linking expedites transformation. Use your imagination the best that you can. The stronger the feeling, the better.

Example of a Positive Affirmation Journal Entry:

"I am aware. I am present. I am flowing. I am controlled. I am purposeful. I am humorous. I am witty. I am honest. I am loyal. I am grateful. I am compassionate. I am energetic. I am magnetic. I am friendly. I am open. I am approachable. I am assertive. I am attentive. I am poised. I am patient. I am serene. I am calm. I am strong. I am fit. I am conscientious. I am imaginative. I am confident. I am charismatic. I am centered. I am grounded. I am disciplined. I am dedicated. I am determined."

These positive affirmations are just examples to get you thinking. The positive affirmations that you choose should be in alignment with the version of your ideal self. This version of your ideal self cannot be determined by anyone but you. Only you know who you are at your core, and who you truly want to be.

By relentlessly focusing on the character traits that you've chosen, you move toward gaining the ability to live life without a filter, as the expression of your true authentic self. The beauty of this entire process is that you are in complete control of who you become. You are the builder of yourself, and only you have the power to decide who you show up in life as.

Strengthening the Connection to Your Conscience

What does this have to do with porn use recovery? Even though my porn problem was mild, I was still using it as a way to escape my reality. See, we all have this little voice inside us that tells us either to do something, or not do something. We call this voice our conscience.

When we watch porn, that little voice whispers "ehhhh you probably shouldn't be doing this." But we watch anyway because we believe that there aren't any consequences for doing so. And that couldn't be further from the truth. I spent years ignoring that little voice that told me I shouldn't watch porn. Those years were the unhappiest years of my life.

The most interesting thing is that since I ignored that voice when it came to using porn, I then ignored it in virtually every other aspect of my life. During the years that I used porn, my life was full of destructive habits that pushed back against my conscience. This created tremendous inner turmoil subconsciously, and fueled my desire to escape.

However, when I stopped watching internet porn, a natural consequence was that I began to listen to my conscience. As you listen to your conscience, its influence is clarified. That would explain how once I stopped watching internet porn, virtually all of my other poor habits simply fell away, and I was able to transcend them almost effortlessly. I quit smoking pot cold turkey, quit binge drinking, stopped complaining, stopped gossiping, cleaned up my diet, began reading everyday, and also added a bunch of other habits to my lifestyle, all of which I share with you in this book.

Where does writing in a journal fit into this equation? Writing in a journal is a way of communicating on a deeper, subconscious level with your conscience. It is a way to gain clarity that cannot be gained in any other way. Then, when you act on your insights, and follow that little voice, you end up transcending most forms of suffering, and you achieve a sense of profound inner peace. This happens because by listening to your conscience, you're acting in alignment with your true nature of being.

When you're out of touch with your true nature of being, you constantly battle yourself. Battling yourself in this way is painful, and never ending. It is a battle that you *cannot* win. So in essence, by journaling every day, you are building your relationship with yourself on the deepest level possible.

As you forge this relationship, you become stronger and stronger, and things that bothered you in the past no longer have power over you. This relationship with your inner being is a bond that supplies you with the strength to quit using porn once and for all. It supplements your will-power, and pulls you forward even in the hardest of times.

However, this doesn't mean that you won't ever feel pain, misery, confusion, or any other negative emotion. It simply means that you'll have created space between you and these emotions. This means that you're better equipped to deal with them as they arise. This space between you and your emotions stop you from identifying with them. This space helps to preserve your sense of self.

The space between you and your emotions allow negative emotions to pass by much faster than if you were still identifying with them. Along with the quicker passing of negative emotions, you gain the ability to honor positive emotions. By honoring positive emotions, you improve your ability to sustain higher moods for longer periods of time. You're then be able to effortlessly savor emotions such as joy, wonder, love, and compassion.

This freedom is what it feels like to live life as an expression of your authentic self. And living life as an expression of your authentic self is what it means to become *A Brand New You.*

CHAPTER 23

The 4th Pillar of Change | Super-Socialization | Cultivating a Sense of Belonging

---

"A deep sense of love and belonging is an irreducible need of all women, men, and children. We are biologically, cognitively, physically, and spiritually wired to love, to be loved."

Brene Brown

The 4th Pillar of Change is super-socialization. It's quite common for regular users of internet porn to feel a sense of social anxiety on a daily basis. I've experienced this in the past, even though I've always been a highly social person. Regardless of whether you're an introvert or an extrovert, porn use causes social anxiety.

Social anxiety evaporates after a month or two of abstaining from using porn. However, this doesn't mean that our social skills are up to par. Even after an extended period of time of porn-free living, we're often left with a weak set of social skills. Under developed social skills are caused by prolonged porn use, usually years, where the individual perpetually avoided social interactions. This avoidance stunts the development of the ability to interact fluidly in social situations.

If not proactively developed, poor social skills can negatively affect many areas of your life. Without sound social skills, virtually all of your relationships remain very surface level. Weak social skills act as a glass ceiling that prevents you from deepening current relationships, as well as making it hard to form new ones.

Humans are social beings. We have an innate desire to feel that we belong. We have a need to feel that we're part of something. If we have poor social skills, like those left in the wake of the exile of internet porn, we often have a hard time developing the ability to communicate with other people. This blocks us from gaining the sense of belonging I am referring to.

What I want you to take from this section is the importance of adopting the mindset of being super-social. What I mean by being super-social is very simple: smile and be friendly to every person that you interact with throughout your day. This means saying hi to everyone. Acknowledge everyone whom you come across in your travels.

Simply smiling and saying hello is powerful. Doing this consistently will help you to baby-step your way to a stronger set of social skills. And don't be discouraged if not everyone responds back to you. The important thing is that you maintain a friendly attitude regardless of how people react. This is a great way to develop yourself socially without being overwhelmed. Over time, you will go from struggling in social situations to being able to thrive in them. At first saying hi to everyone will probably feel uncomfortable. But as you carry on, your level of comfort will increase naturally.

You will find that as you change how you look at the world, the world changes how it looks at you. By simply saying hi and acknowledging everyone you come across, you open the door to grow your social skills in the most natural way possible. People will become attracted to you because of your friendly nature. They will enjoy your presence, and look forward to talking with you. As this happens, your social skills will continue to improve and your interactions will deepen from just saying hi, to sustained genuine conversation.

This sense of growth will help you feel good about yourself, and help you to gain a sense of belonging in the world. This positive feedback will encourage you to keep expanding your comfort zone. With repetition, you'll find that social skills are not that hard to develop. You'll find that it just takes time and consistency to improve. You'll also find that it's a lot of fun.

By adopting this mindset of being super-social, your current relationships will deepen, and you'll make many new friends. This healthy cultivation of your social life will have a profound effect on your self-esteem, confidence, and overall attitude towards life. And remember, the better you feel, the less likely you'll be to revert back to an old porn habit. And with improved self-esteem and confidence, you have what you need to go talk to that pretty girl that you see every day on your way to work. Don't waste any more time. The clock is ticking. Remember that you miss 100% of the shots you don't take. Get out there, and start living. Start being super-social today!

Simple Tips for Better Social Interactions

1. Strong eye contact
2. Stand up straight
3. Be a great listener
4. Don't fidget
5. Don't fold your arms
6. Don't put hands in your pockets
7. Feel the ground under your feet
8. Breathe deeply, and relax

CHAPTER 24

The 5th Pillar of Change | Social Media DETOX | Dropping Comparison & Judgement

---

"A day spent judging another is a painful day. A day judging yourself is a painful day."

Buddha

The 5th Pillar of Change is social media DETOX. While the topic of socializing is on our minds, let's shift our focus to social media. In a world where technology is moving faster with each passing day, we are burdened with the task of continuously adapting to keep up. Sometimes on the surface, these advancements seem to be beneficial. Then, only after long term use are we able to gain clarity of the drawbacks. Sometimes it takes years before we realize the negative effects of certain technology.

Social media is an incredible tool, and there are many benefits for utilizing it. It has the power to connect the world all on one platform, where we can share ideas, causes, and connect with people in a way that was not possible prior to its creation. However, social media is one form of technology that can be very damaging to our well-being if we don't use it mindfully.

Everyday there are new studies that link social media use with depression and anxiety. It is finally common knowledge that excessive social media use is not helping us live happy and fulfilling lives.

At the most fundamental level, using social media is an anti-social activity. Communicating through a screen is a low, base level substitute for person-to-person interaction. Slowly but surely, social media is making us anti-social creatures. All you have to do is look around to see this. Everyone is literally attached to their cell phones at all times, constantly checking, posting, liking, following, and viewing on Instagram, Facebook, Twitter, Snapchat and countless other social media platforms. That said, social media is more suited to be classified as anti-social media.

Using social media as a replacement for real life socialization can cause many problems beyond both depression and anxiety. It also can stunt the growth of our social skills, and isolate us in real life due to the increasing lack of face-to-face human interaction that is common among frequent social media users. The constant flood of high-light reel posts triggers constant judgement and comparison, which leaves us feeling like our lives are boring and inadequate. This never-ending game of comparison leads to constant striving to keep up, without ever feeling like we are good enough, regardless of what we post. This inevitable comparison causes us to form judgements of others, and can also lead to strong feelings of jealousy and resentment. The negative impact social media has on our well-being combined with the fact that these social media platforms are also designed to be addictive, and we are in serious trouble. Being addicted to comparison and judgement is a recipe for disaster. Their addictive design and fascinating novelty entice us to use over and over again, regardless of the negative consequences. If we are truly serious about living a happy life, we have to open our eyes to how this technology is impacting our personal well-being, and ask ourselves if it's worth it.

The negative impact of social media on our well-being is an important realization to understand in both life, and on our quest to quit internet porn use. With a shift in our perception, we can use what we've learned to our advantage. By purposefully and mindfully adjusting the way that we use social media, we can effectively avoid the detrimental impact, and still gain from the benefits. And by avoiding things such as depression, anxiety, isolation, jealousy, resentment, and continuous judgement; we increase our chance of maintaining a high mood and steady positive emotional state that we work so hard to cultivate through the proactive design of our lifestyle. Our overall goal is simple; feel as good as possible as much as possible, because when you feel good, you're less likely to revert to using porn.

One other way the mindful use of social media helps us in our quest to quit internet porn, is that by staying off social media you avoid triggers. A trigger may be a promiscuous, half-naked picture of an Instagram model, or a video from a crazy college party with multiple girls making out in bikinis.

If you're familiar with the social media landscape, particularly Instagram, you know that these two examples are a very common find. The problem is that you never know what posts will appear on your news feed. It's out of your control. You're literally at the mercy of pure chance in regards to what pops up. If you allow yourself to be at the mercy of pure chance, you aren't giving yourself the best chance for a successful recovery from porn use.

Many of the men that I mentor online report being triggered by a random sexual picture or video on social media. It's common that they trace their strong urge to view porn to random exposure to sexual imagery. We can avoid this undesired scenario all together by simply committing to the adjustment of the way that we use social media.

If you're serious about quitting porn and achieving lasting self-transformation, temporarily quitting social media simultaneously is very helpful. I would go as far to say that it's an extremely vital step in manifesting true self-transformation. However, we don't have to delete all of our social media accounts to make this change.

My strategy for what I call a social media DETOX, is to limit your social media use to computer use only. This means to take all of your social media apps off of your smartphone. The reason for this is to avoid mindless use throughout your day. This eliminates mindless distractions, and the constant fragmentation of your focus. I recommend giving yourself one free pass per month, or per week, to check your social media accounts from a computer. This allows you to still remain "connected" in a sense, but not to the extent that it's detrimental to your personal well-being. You'll be astonished by the overall improvement in your mood, as well as its sustainability, when you fully commit to this Social Media DETOX.

I was an avid social media user for many years prior to implementing this strategy. If you would have asked me at the peak of my social media use if I was happy, I would have told you that of course I am happy. However, the contrast in how I feel now, compared to when I was using social media mindlessly every single day, is not even comparable. Because of this stark contrast, I feel that much of the negative impact of social media occurs at a sub-conscious level, just like the impact of using porn. This is dangerous to our well-being because we don't realize the damage that's being done. We only make this realization when we remove it from our lives, and then reflect on how we feel.

Quitting excessive everyday use of social media was one of the most important decisions I have ever made. My life has improved on so many levels naturally, without much effort. My focus and concentration are improved and my mind is sharper. I'm effortlessly able to stay present to the moment. I am non-judgmental of both myself and others, and I enjoy social interactions more than ever. My relationships have thrived, and I have a dramatically increased value for the time I spend face-to-face with friends and family. I just feel marvelous.

That said, make a social media DETOX a part of your life, and see how things change. If you don't feel any difference, you can always go back to your old ways. But you'll never know how enjoyable life can be without social media until you take some time away from it, and see how the break makes you feel. If you're recovering from a porn habit, these positive changes catalyzed by a social media DETOX will greatly increase your ability to successfully quit your internet porn use, and live a more meaningful life in the process.

CHAPTER 25

The 6th Pillar of Change | Passion Pursuits | Eliminating Boredom

---

"Passion is energy. Feel the power that comes from focusing on what excites you."

Oprah Winfrey

The 6th Pillar of Change is passion pursuits. Boredom is a major cause for relapse among recovering porn users. One way to minimize boredom in your life is to refocus a portion of your time and energy on doing something that you have passion for. This may be a hobby such as mountain biking, tennis, the guitar, or reading classic literature. The important thing is that you are proactively taking action to pour your heart and energy into something you love.

Doing this not only makes you feel great, but it also fills up blocks of time that you may have used in the past for surfing internet porn tube sites. Many men who quit using porn report that once they stop using, they suddenly have huge blocks of free time. The men that relapse most often are the ones who remain stagnant, and don't make good use of this new free time. So take up a new hobby or revive an old passion. Don't allow yourself to sit around and be bored.

It's also highly likely that once you begin to build up a reserve of sexual energy, that you'll feel the need to get moving. You'll feel the need to use that stored up energy in any way that you can. My advice is to combine the proactive development of yourself with pursuits of passion. Do things that you love. Do things that excite you. Do things that energize you. Pour your heart into something that fills you up, and adds meaning to your life.

For me, I made the commitment to revive my competitive golf career. Before my decision to quit using porn, I had been away from professional golf for almost four years. At that time, my golf game was non-existent and my skills were terrible. But once I decided to get back into it, I used my built up energy to retool my game, and revive a passion that had given me so much over the years.

My drive to improve as a golfer has given me added purpose to remain dedicated to my decision to quit using porn. At this point in my life, porn is long gone. But early on in my journey, having something to pour my energy into was critical. In hindsight, this passion pursuit was vital for my long term recovery.

Begin a new passion pursuit or revive an old one, and use it for added purpose to transcend porn. There is no telling how far a passion pursuit will take you. Throw some wood on the fire, and let it rage. There's no better time to add some passion to your life than right now.

CHAPTER 26

The 7th Pillar of Change | Motivational Material | Powering through the Dreaded Flatline

---

"If you can't fly, then run, if you can't run, then walk, if you can't walk, then crawl, but whatever you do you have to keep moving forward."

Martin Luther King Jr.

What is the flatline? The flatline is a mysteriously scary period of time during a reboot from porn when a man feels that he has lost all function of his sexual gear, and that his libido has perished. Many men also report low mood and low motivation during this time.

The dreaded flatline can strike at any time during a reboot. However, most men experience this during the first 3-5 weeks of quitting porn use. But it's also important to note that some men report flatlines after multiple months of being porn-free. Some men even report multiple flatlines per reboot. The flatline seems to vary greatly between individuals attempting to quit porn use.

For someone unfamiliar with the flatline, this time period can be unsettling. Many guys describe their genitals as feeling lifeless, and cold. This can cause a man to panic, because he is afraid of losing the function of his penis, which often leads him to revert to porn in order to "make sure that it still works."

Relapsing to "make sure that it still works" can be paralyzing, because it compounds the pain. It's like adding insult to injury, and it only makes things much worse. Relapsing during flatline is like rubbing salt in a fresh wound. You want to stay away from falling into this trap at all costs. The flatline seems to be a withdrawal symptom unique to quitting porn use, and there's no proven reason why some of us experience it. All we can do, is prepare for the worst, and hope for the best.

However, not all men experience the flatline. Personally, I can't put my finger on a specific point in time where I went through a flatline. I don't know why, but I speculate that since my porn use was mild, I was able to reboot without a flatline.

I also have a hunch that my relentless campaign to add healthy habits to my lifestyle prevented me from ever dipping into a flatline. For example, in the first month of my reboot, I began mindfulness meditation twice per day, daily weight training, as well as writing in a journal in both the morning and night. I believe that these habits kept me buoyant throughout my quest to quit porn, and made my journey much easier than it otherwise would have been.

That said, if you're just starting out on your own journey, I suggest that you put your best effort into incorporating these same habits into your lifestyle. Get really serious about it. Don't skip out on anything. Being relentlessly proactive will give you the best chance at both avoiding a flatline, and a full recovery.

But what do you do if you're experiencing a flatline right this very moment? Well, I tell all of the men that I mentor to lean on their self-discipline. Just because you don't feel motivated doesn't mean you can't take action. I urge them to man up, and muster the strength to get moving.

Take massive action. Hit the gym, meditate, write in your journal, or go for a long walk; just do anything but stay still. Don't allow your emotions to paralyze you. If you allow yourself to stagnate, it's only a matter of time before you think about relapsing to escape the discomfort.

Your brain will rationalize in funny ways to get you to escape sadness and despair. Before you know it, you'll be opening your internet browser typing in the name of your favorite porn tube site. Avoid this at all costs by forcing yourself to get moving by exercising your self-discipline! If you relapse, you'll only feel much worse. Avoid feeling much worse by immediately taking action in the moment. Just know that if you relapse, that pain is coming for your ass, and there's no stopping it.

However, there is a way to help yourself ascend from that lowly state, and trigger some motivation that can help you to gain some forward momentum. I've found that anytime I have lacked motivation or drive, or felt a little down, I benefit greatly from motivational material. I use the term motivational material loosely because it comes in many different forms; books, music, audio, or video.

Using motivational material can help to snap your physiology out of a lowly state. My favorite form of motivational material is in the form of audio/video on YouTube. There are thousands of awesome motivational videos on YouTube that you can utilize to spark inspiration.

Open up YouTube and type "motivational videos" into the search bar and thousands of choices will pop up. Choose one, and see if it resonates with you. If not, close it and try another. Repeat this process until you find one that you like. Listen to it, and feel your body come to life. Feel the energy that this positive material catalyzes within you. Five of my favorite YouTube channels that offer super-charged motivation are *Mulligan Brothers*, *Be Inspired*, *Absolute Motivation*, *Motivation Archive*, and *Video Advice*. These channels really bring the heat when it comes to motivation! Check them out!

Listen to these motivational videos at the same time that you force yourself to take action. I feel like a warrior going into battle when I do this. It's a tremendously powerful and energizing feeling to take action in the face of adversity. It's even more powerful if you have a coach (motivational video), pushing you forward. Before you know it, you'll be surging with energy, determined to not let anything stop you from achieving your goals in life.

You can use this same strategy with your favorite music. If I feel like I need something other than a motivational video, I'll fire up some Logic to get my blood pumping. I'm a huge fan of Logic and I love all of his music, but my go-to songs are *Under Pressure, Run It, The Jam, Flexicution, Contra, Wizard of Oz, Everybody*, and *Yuck.*

This self-coaching tactic is extremely useful any time you feel unmotivated. However, they're also great to listen to when you're feeling great. I listen to motivational videos or my favorite music during every drive to the gym. This is extremely helpful to program my mind with positive, encouraging, and inspirational thoughts that prime my mind for domination.

My travel time to the gym is also only 10 minutes, which is proof that it doesn't take long to snap yourself into a highly motivated state. Doing this on a regular basis helps to build up your motivational muscle. With repetition it becomes much easier to both snap yourself into a positive mind state, and sustain that state for a longer period of time. Utilize this energy building tactic on a daily basis, and you'll be well on your way to launching out of that flatline, and into a mind state for domination in the face of challenge.

CHAPTER 27

The 8th Pillar of Change | Relapse Remedies | The Power of Shifted Focus

---

"Where focus goes, energy flows."

Tony Robbins

Urges to relapse are inevitable, especially early on in the recovery from porn use. There are a few tricks that can help you neutralize the urge to relapse. The three best ways to neutralize the strong primal urge to relapse are to get physically moving, go to where there are people, or clean your living space. I call this trio, *Relapse Remedies.*

The first *Relapse Remedy* is to get up and get moving. This means to literally, get up and get moving. Try doing push-ups, crunches, go to the gym to work out, or go outside and take a walk. My go-to has always been a nice long walk in nature. Spending time outdoors is a great way to quiet the mind, and refresh the spirit.

But what you actually do doesn't really matter. The most important thing is that you immediately take initiative to get moving. By becoming physically active you literally change your physiology, and create the proper conditions to allow the sexual urge to pass peacefully.

The second *Relapse Remedy* is to go where there are people. This may mean going to hang out with your parents, a sibling, a roommate, or maybe even taking a drive to the coffee shop down the street. The reason for this is obvious; you can't watch porn and be around people at the same time. I mean, you could. But doing so would have extremely negative consequences, like going to jail. Nobody wants to go to jail.

So put yourself in the presence of other people to take your mind off of the urge to relapse. It may also help to talk to someone, so be super-social. Use your energy productively by expressing it socially. Socializing will help you shift your focus away from the urge, and onto something that requires your attention; a real person. Engaging in social interactions will help to keep your focus occupied for the time it takes for the urge to pass. And you'll maybe even make a friend or two in the process.

The third *Relapse Remedy* is to clean and organize your living space. Most of the time when the unexpected porn urge hits us, it's because we're in a state of stagnation. If you recognize this right away, all you have to do is get moving.

Act instead of think. It can be extremely helpful to look around your living space and see if there's any cleaning, or tidying up that can be done.

Tidying up your living space takes your focus off of the urge, and moves it to the task of analyzing your surroundings. You might decide that your bedroom needs to be dusted, trash needs to be emptied, or that your bookshelf needs organizing.

Regardless of what you choose to do, the most important thing is that you get started on it right away. Get active in completing whatever task you've chosen. You may have to repeat this process for as long as it takes to be consciously aware that the sexual urge has passed. This kills two birds with one stone. You will have kept your streak of porn-free living alive, and you will have improved your living space in the process.

Next time you feel an urge, choose one of these three methods to refocus your attention elsewhere, and stick to it until you feel that the urge has passed. Be patient with yourself. Act deliberately, but take your time. Even the strongest of urges go away eventually.

CHAPTER 28

The 9th Pillar of Change | Cold Shower Therapy | Compounded Will-Power

---

"In any given moment we have two options: to step forward into growth or to step back into safety."

Abraham Maslow

The 9th Pillar of Change is cold shower therapy. Cold showers are one of the most popular ways for killing a porn urge, but more importantly developing increased will-power. Cold shower therapy helps you to become comfortable with uncomfortable situations. I mean think about it, who really enjoys taking an ice cold shower? I've been taking cold showers for a long time, and for the first 20 seconds they stick suck. What doesn't suck is how you feel once you get out. And what's even better is the strengthening of your will-power that's forged in the process. Cold showers help to build tremendous will-power and resolve.

Cold showers are among the most popular life hacks of people attempting to quit their porn habit. Many of the men I mentor utilize this technique as their number one way of avoiding relapse. Nothing quite kills that sexual urge like ice cold water.

Along with putting out a flame of lustful desire, there's a myriad of positive health benefits associated with taking regular cold showers. The health benefits of cold shower therapy are improved circulation, healthier hair and skin, improved mood, and a super-charged energy boost. Cold showers have also been proven to alleviate depression. By taking cold showers, you open the door for many health benefits that contribute to higher well-being.

It's important to note that the length of time you spend in a cold shower doesn't affect the benefits. My best advice is to shoot for a minimum of one minute, and a maximum three minutes. Anywhere within that time frame is sufficient to experience the desired positive benefits. Of course, you can be an absolute savage and stay in for as long as you'd like, but a long cold shower isn't really necessary.

My strategy for making cold shower therapy a concrete habit, is to imbed it into your morning routine. The reason for this is so every morning as soon as you wake up, you know that you're going to start your day with a cold shower. Imbedding it into a routine helps to remove any further decision making as to when you should, or shouldn't take one.

Your brain will rationalize reasons to avoid discomfort, and by having a scheduled time for your cold shower therapy, you avoid that rationalization altogether. Another reason for starting your day with a cold shower is because it's incredibly powerful to step into discomfort very early on in your day. Cold showers first thing in the morning help you to become super-charged for the rest of your day.

As for when you're actually in the cold shower, focus on breathing deeply. At first, the cold water will cause shallow breathing. Do your best to relax, and breathe as deep as you can. Imagine your breath traveling all the way down into your feet, and out the bottom of your heels. This deep breathing can be difficult at first, but with practice you'll improve. Taking at least one cold shower a day will change your life.

I feel like a Spartan warrior ready for battle every time I step out of a cold shower. It's awesome. I'm ready to take on any challenge life throws at me. You too can start the day feeling like a warrior by taking just one cold shower every single day.

CHAPTER 29

The 10th Pillar of Change | Floatation Therapy | Floating to Freedom

---

"The sensory deprivation chamber is the most important tool I've ever used for developing my mind for thinking, for evolving."

Joe Rogan

The 10th Pillar of Change is floatation therapy. Contrary to the popularity of cold shower therapy, floatation therapy is the least known tool for porn use recovery. Floatation therapy is the use of an isolation tank, sensory deprivation chamber, or float tank. Floatation therapy is a new form of holistic healing that has been proven to help people recover from various forms of addiction. That said, floating can be of great use to anyone looking to quit porn, especially those with extreme porn addictions.

The general idea is to float inside an enclosed tank that's filled with about 10 inches of warm water, and over 1000 pounds of pharmaceutical grade Epsom salts. The water's temperature is skin receptor neutral so as time passes you lose feeling of where the water meets your skin, and the Epsom salts keep you buoyant, which causes you to float effortlessly. Most float spas offer sessions of one to three hours. One hour is the best length for beginners.

Float tanks usually have interior lighting, but traditional floating is done in complete darkness. These tanks are usually sound proof as well. The float experience is designed to eliminate all distractions. Floating offers the rare opportunity to completely unplug from the hyperactivity that we deal with every single day. Inside the float tank, it's just you and your thoughts. This slice of solitude is one of the most relaxing and valuable experiences that I know of for recharging your mind, body, and spirit.

My best advice for first-time floaters is to go into the experience with no expectations. Do your best to take things slow, and relax. Allow yourself to just be. Do your best to completely let go. Whatever you experience in the tank is perfect for you in that particular moment.

In the beginning, usually the first 15-20 minutes, your mind will bounce around from thought to thought, but eventually everything will slow down. It's this profound relaxation that replenishes the mind, body, and spirit like nothing else can. If you don't experience this depth of relaxation in your first float, don't worry. It's normal to need to float a few times before you're able to be fully absorbed in the experience. Be patient with yourself. All of the best things in life take time.

It's also important to understand that not much happens inside the tank. The magic happens when you get out of the tank, and rejoin the real world. Life takes on a new meaning. Colors are sharper, nature is more vibrant, and the miracles of life become quite obvious. It's really hard to describe. You have to feel the power of floating for yourself to fully understand it. I've fallen in love with floating, and it continues to get better the more I do it. So what are you waiting for? Try it out! Give it some time, and I'm confident it'll change your life just as it has for me.

But let's talk more about the benefits. Floating boosts your mood by increasing dopamine and endorphin levels naturally, while simultaneously reducing stress by minimizing cortisol production. It induces a deep meditative state that's difficult to be achieved anywhere else. Floating also helps to relieve symptoms of depression, anxiety, PTSD, Crohn's, and Parkinson's disease. I have Crohn's disease, and floating has allowed me to live a much more normal life. If you're interested in learning more about floating, check out the informative and eye-opening documentary, *Float Nation,* on YouTube.

The biggest drawback of floating is that takes time. A one hour float session can take up to two hours from the time you walk into the spa until the time you leave, considering the time it takes to shower and clean up before and after your float. This is a challenge because our lives are busier than ever, and we're constantly being pulled at from all angles. The constant demand on our time makes it challenging to find the couple hours that it takes to go float.

However, there's good news. It's been proven that the positive benefits of floating can be maintained for weeks after just one session. That means we can maintain the many benefits by floating on just an occasional basis. Obviously, the ideal situation is to float as much as possible. But floating once in a while is now proven to be better than not floating at all. I can attest to this because I'm able to maintain feeling absolutely awesome by floating for just one hour, once per month. But if I am overdue for a float, I can feel it. I can feel when it's time to schedule a session, and this feeling arises if I wait any longer than four weeks between floats.

Shout out to my go-to float center, *Euphoria Float Spa*. If you're ever in Western Mass, check them out. They're the best.

That brings us to our next challenge: accessing a float center. The float industry is still relatively new. Most float centers are found exclusively in busy metropolitan areas. That means that there's a pretty good chance that there isn't a float center within a reasonable distance from where you live. However, if there isn't a center nearby, there are a few things you can do to simulate the float setting in the comfort of your own home. It's pretty simple too- just take a bath or shower in complete darkness.

You won't achieve the same amount of health benefits as floating, but you'll experience a decent degree of peaceful solitude. I use this simulation strategy at the end of my day, almost every day. The darkness and solitude help me to stimulate my imagination, creativity, and helps me disconnect. That said, if you do have access to a float center, take advantage of it. But if you can't float for whatever reason, you can still benefit from simulating a float session.

An important reminder- be careful when doing anything in the dark, and be mindful of the location of your light switch to avoid slipping and falling when your simulated float session is complete. A low-brightness night light is a good investment to avoid any type of accident.

CHAPTER 30

The 11th Pillar of Change | Rituals | Two Routines for Routine Growth

---

"The secret to your future is hidden in your daily routine."

Mike Murdock

If you can win the morning, you can win the day. A strong morning routine gets you going on the right foot. It helps you to start the day with a sense of accomplishment, and fuels optimism for what's to come. A strong nightly routine is no different. A nightly routine allows you to process the events and emotions of the day, and gives you a sense of closure. It can also help clear out mental baggage, and help to highlight your progress in life. A clear mind from a strong nightly routine will also help you to achieve higher quality sleep, and a deeper rest increases your effectiveness the following day.

At first, these routines may feel tedious and burdensome. However, with persistence you'll grow to enjoy them as you experience the added value that these routines bring to your life. As time passes, your morning and nightly routines become the cornerstones of your day, and they help you to operate as efficiently and effectively as possible.

We all lead very different lives, which means that these routines will be different for each individual. What works well for me, may not work for you. And what works for you, might not work for your friend. There's no wrong way to structure your morning and nightly routines. Do your best to keep an open mind for experimentation. Explore what works best for your life situation and daily commitments. Pay close attention to how you feel when you're experimenting, and stick to what feels good. Follow what energizes you, and be sure to design your routines for what makes sense for your lifestyle.

Regardless of what your routines consist of, the most important thing to focus on, is that you get in the habit of repeating them every single day. It takes repetition before you're able to perform them like clockwork. The beginning of any type of behavior change is always where the most difficulty lies.

There'll certainly be days when you feel like skipping your routines. It's in these moments where you have the opportunity to make the most progress. Going against what you feel like doing exercises your discipline. As your discipline becomes stronger, you're less affected by your emotions. Your discipline eventually becomes so strong that you become unstoppable. The gains from this level of discipline are limitless.

Increased discipline then affects your self-image and you begin to see yourself as someone who gets shit done no matter the circumstances. This is the warrior mentality. This discipline driven mentality then bleeds into all other areas of your life, and you gain massive power over your behavior.

Once you get a taste of this warrior mentality, there's no going back. Once a warrior, always a warrior. The warrior mentality is what separates people who achieve their goals from people who dream about achieving them. Strong self-discipline drives achievement, and strong morning and nightly routines breed unbreakable self-discipline.

The idea of a strong morning and nightly routine is not new. I adopted this strategy from Napoleon Hill's book *Think and Grow Rich.* He stresses the importance of having a strong routine for both the morning and night as a strategy for programming the subconscious mind with pre-determined thoughts about the goals that you want to achieve. This is the same reason why I believe having a strong morning and nightly routine is vital for consistent personal growth.

By utilizing these two windows of time to program the subconscious mind with desired thoughts related to personal goals and character development, you maximize your ability to transform. When you go to bed at night, you'll be consciously asleep, but your subconscious mind will be steady working on solutions for achieving your desired goals.

These two windows of time, right when we wake up and right before we go to sleep, are the doorways to the subconscious mind. It's well known that the subconscious mind is immensely more powerful than the conscious mind. Because of this, our subconscious controls a majority of how we think, feel, and act. By proactively tapping into the power of the subconscious mind by utilizing these two windows of time, we're able to make change occur at a rapid pace. This strategy catalyzes transformation faster than otherwise possible.

There are only two musts when constructing an effective morning and nightly routine. These musts are meditation, and writing in a journal. These two activities are the foundation of strong morning and nightly routines because they're the most effective activities for influencing the subconscious mind. Meditation calms the mind, and writing reprograms it. The subconscious is also most receptive at the time right when you wake up, and right before you fall asleep. That said, it's crucial to take advantage of these windows of opportunity.

You can also add other beneficial activities like cold showers, reading, creative work, or exercise to these routines. Be creative, and see what works best for you. Experiment to see what energizes you, and helps you to function at your highest level.

These routines will vary between individuals. The important thing to figure out is what works best for you, and to stick with it for as long as it remains working. However, keep an open mind, and be aware of how these routines make you feel. As your life situation and daily commitments change, don't be afraid to switch things up and try something new. Always keep the door open for new ways to improve. Sometimes a small tweak here or there makes all the difference.

Below I share the routines that work really well for me. This is simply an example to get you thinking about how you can begin to structure your own routines. I hope this example helps you gain a better sense of where to start and what to try. You'll also notice that each routine takes a relatively short period of time. Keeping your life situation in mind, you might find that your routines are longer or shorter. You may have more time to allocate in the morning than at night, or vice versa. The amount of time used for each routine is not what's important. What's important is the execution of each routine on an everyday basis. Unwavering execution is the main driver for rapid growth, and profound transformation. Another tip is to not over complicate things. Keep each routine simple enough to avoid overwhelm, but hearty enough to support a deep sense of involvement and concentration.

My Morning Routine:

1. *Journal entry- positive affirmations (15 minutes)*
2. *Guided meditation using the Calm App (15 minutes)*
3. *Cold Shower (5 minutes)*

Total time used: 35 minutes

My Nightly Routine:

1. *Read at least 1 Chapter of a book of choice (20 minutes)*
2. *Guided meditation using the Calm App (15 minutes)*
3. *Journal entry- free write (15 minutes)*

Total time used: 50 minutes

PART III: The Attitude to Evolve

"Your attitude, not your aptitude,
will determine your altitude."

Zig Ziglar

CHAPTER 31

The Importance of an Optimistic Attitude | Your Shield against Failure

---

"A positive attitude causes a chain reaction of positive thoughts, events, and outcomes. It is a catalyst and it sparks extraordinary results."

Wade Boggs

Achieving the results that you desire greatly depend on your ability to keep a stable, optimistic attitude toward life. Optimism helps you to feel better about yourself, better about your progress toward your goal of quitting porn, and also helps you bounce back after setbacks. Having a positive attitude also reinforces the belief in your plan for change, which helps to strengthen your commitment. A strong commitment level then births a high level a discipline and consistency in carrying out the actions associated with that plan, because the rewards of your commitment are clear and exciting. This excitement keeps you focused, and helps to maintain your forward momentum.

A positive attitude energizes you, and keeps you focused on what you need to do to get where you want to go. This is crucial for being able to navigate the sometimes rough waters of self-transformation. When you're striving to change yourself, it isn't all fun and games. Having an optimistic outlook on life in times of difficulty helps to maintain your belief in what's possible for yourself, even when it feels like your world is crumbling in on you.

Being positive also keeps you motivated because you can see the light at the end of the tunnel. The light at the end of the tunnel represents how your life is improving as a result of sticking to your plan of action. The more optimistic you are, the brighter the light. The strength of this light pulls you ahead like a magnet. This positive force streamlines progress, and gets you to the attainment of your goals quicker than if you employed a negative attitude.

A positive attitude pulls you forward toward your future visions of yourself and your life. A negative attitude pushes back against you. Negativity is resistance that fuels self-doubt, and self-doubt is the killer of all dreams. We all have to deal with self-doubt at times; it's a fact of life.

However, nurturing an optimistic mindset helps to stop doubt in its tracks. By recognizing the moment of doubt, and refocusing on the positive, you can shake it off and get back to business. If you maintain a negative mindset, doubt persists. Then, your negative mindset continues to fuel the doubt, much like a brisk wind fuels a forest fire. As your sense of doubt grows stronger, your brain rationalizes reasons to give up. Giving up is not an option.

Doubt will do everything in its power to push you off course. Achievement in life is demanding. It can be difficult enough with a positive mindset. Don't make it harder on yourself than it has to be. Let go of the negativity, and train yourself to focus on the positive of every situation. A positive outlook on life is vital for breaking through perceived limits. Just when it looks like things have gone terribly wrong, you can refocus your energy on the positive, and do everything that you possibly can to push through. Just beyond the pain lies the gold.

However, if you surrender to self-doubt, you'll never know what it feels like to truly transform. You'll never know what it feels like to break free from past vices, and become the person you've always known you could be.

Think of an optimistic attitude as your shield against failure. Think of it as your insurance policy for success. Failure only happens when you give up on yourself, and giving up on yourself only happens when you allow self-doubt to rule your mental landscape. By cultivating and maintaining an attitude of optimism, you can protect yourself from doubt and negativity. When you fearlessly wield the shield of optimism, there's nothing that can't be achieved.

CHAPTER 32

Maintaining Life Balance | Navigating the Land of Lust

"Life is like riding a bicycle. To keep your balance, you must keep moving."

Albert Einstein

Throughout your journey from porn to freedom, much of your success will depend on your ability to maintain healthy life balance. This life balance spans across the entire spectrum of your life. You must remain balanced in mind, body, and spirit. The more balanced you become, the easier you will sustain the success of your recovery. However, life is messy by nature, and it can be easy to fall out of balance. This is expected and natural. It happens to all of us. The important thing to remember when we become aware of an imbalance is what we need to do to offset it. Awareness is key for being able to take the necessary steps to get back into a balanced state.

When we fall out of balance in any of these three areas, we become susceptible to reverting back to our old porn habit that we've worked so hard to quit. Combined with porn's ease of access, and the excessive sexual world that we live in, and standing strong against those urges becomes much more difficult.

For this reason, it's imperative to keep a very close watch on how you feel in respect to your mind, body and spirit. You have to become the watcher of yourself. Only you will be able to notice the most acute changes, and this keen awareness makes all the difference. Your ability to tune into what's going on within, and your ability to act accordingly, greatly increases your chances of successfully quitting porn for good.

When you feel like you're slipping, stop and refocus on what you can do to counteract that imbalance. It may mean sitting to meditate, going to work out, writing in your journal, or meeting a friend out for lunch. The ability to think on your feet and act proactively in the face of uncertainty is crucial for getting yourself back into a balanced state of being. Maintaining a healthy life balance is incredibly important for consistently feeling great, and feeling great is what keeps us from going back to bad habits.

CHAPTER 33

The Relapse | Befriending Setbacks

"Success is not final, failure is not fatal: it is the courage to continue that counts."

Winston Churchill

The most interesting dynamic about internet porn addiction is how it's unlike most other addictions. The porn itself is intangible, and essentially free to access. Given its overwhelming presence on the internet, it's something that we can very easily go back to if we don't design our lives in a manner that allow us to be proactively participating in the development of ourselves at a high level.

I've learned that the reality is that everyone who struggles with internet pornography use will have many relapses before they're able to quit for a long enough time to be fully healed. I have yet to meet someone who uses on a regular basis, and succeeds cold turkey on their first attempt to quit.

Relapses are simply a part of the game given the circumstances at play. Realizing this makes it much easier to deal with relapses in a positive manner. By avoiding beating ourselves up over a relapse, we can quickly pick ourselves up, and get back to making progress as soon as possible.

It took me many attempts before I was able to put together 30 days straight of porn-free living. The time leading up to this streak was stricken with relapse after relapse. I continually put together streaks of 4, 8, 12, and 15 days, and it wasn't until two months into quitting that I was able to put together a 30 day streak. So even though it seemed like just a mild problem for me, it still required a lot of persistence and determination to kick the habit once and for all.

For someone who's a compulsive addict who watches porn multiple times per day, recovery may be drawn out over a much longer period of time. Many of the young men I mentor online have been struggling with this addiction for years. There's an interesting correlation between age and the time that it takes to permanently quit using porn. The correlation is that younger men have a much harder time quitting porn than men who adopted this bad habit later on in their lives. Older men seem to be able to kick the habit faster, and with more ease.

I can attest to this because I didn't use internet porn until I was 20 years old. That said, my brain had done most of its major development before I started using. So for someone who grew up using internet porn, quitting may take much longer.

Given how powerful this addiction is and the nature of what it takes to fully reboot, it's important to understand that relapses are simply an aspect of recovery. We will all relapse at one point or another.

What matters is that we remain committed to our decision to quit. We have to remind ourselves in the wake of the inevitable relapse that we're still winning, because we're still committed to quitting. We have to remind ourselves that all progress is not lost. We have to remind ourselves that we will eventually win this battle, as long as we continue to pick ourselves up after we fall.

By understanding that relapse is a part of the game, we can avoid being too hard on ourselves when we slip up. The problem with being hard on ourselves is that harsh self-talk often leads to binging. We feel awful because we messed up, and we then convince ourselves that our progress is lost. We then revert back to porn, and go on a binge; rationalizing to ourselves that there's nothing more to lose. We have to avoid this rationalization at all costs.

Relapse is a stepping stone towards our ultimate victory. This perception helps us to avoid identifying with failure, and keeps us from falling into the trap of binge porn use. Anytime we identify with failure, we feed negativity.

This negativity eats away at our commitment, discipline, and momentum. We can't allow ourselves to think in this way, because it blocks us from getting where we need to go.

With time, patience, and persistence, relapsing becomes less frequent. The longer we go without relapsing the stronger and more resilient we become. Eventually, we get to the point where we understand very clearly the tremendous value that quitting porn brings to our life. It's at this point that our journey out from the darkness becomes much easier.

We cannot appreciate the light without the dark, and the good without the bad. The cultivation of persistence and understanding allows us to grow from the inspire stage, into the transformational stage, and finally into the evolve stage, where we know in our heart that we have transcended porn use forever.

CHAPTER 34

What to Do After a Relapse | Acceptance and Gratitude

"Gratitude makes sense of our past, brings peace for today, and creates a vision for tomorrow."

Melody Beattie

It happened. You relapsed. We now understand that we shouldn't beat ourselves up about it, but what do we do now? How do we avoid the dreadful binge, and maintain our positive momentum? There are two steps that you should follow after a relapse to avoid any further setbacks.

Step one is to accept the relapse. There's nothing you can do about it at this point, so you might as well accept it for what it is. Acceptance allows us to leap frog all of the negative emotions on the emotional scale, and brings us to a place of balance, stability and forgiveness.

If we don't practice acceptance during the time right after a relapse, we'll undoubtedly toil with lower level emotions like grief, anger, shame, guilt, sadness, and powerlessness. By accepting what's happened, we avoid judging ourselves. By not judging ourselves, we avoid identifying with failure. We need to do our best to simply accept it for what it is, and move on. By accepting the relapse and refraining from judgement, we take the first step toward regaining our positive momentum.

Step two is to reframe the situation, and view what's happened through a lens of gratitude. I know, it can be challenging to try and find appreciation for any unfortunate event in life. But reframing a relapse with gratitude helps to preserve your commitment.

We then have to revisit our purpose for choosing to quit. We must remind ourselves how quitting is going to make our life experience better. We must remind ourselves that adversity forges strength. By reframing the situation with gratitude, we take the second step toward retaining the progress that we've worked so hard for.

The first few times you relapse, this process of accepting and reframing the situation will be difficult. However, it gets easier with practice. Just keep pushing ahead and stay positive. With perseverance you will prevail.

You can also use this strategy for other negative situations not related to porn relapse. This is a useful strategy to bring with you throughout your life experience. By understanding the importance of acceptance and gratitude, you're armed with the tools to handle any challenge life throws at you.

CHAPTER 35

A Crucial Realization | Post-Sex Vibes vs. Post-Relapse Vibes

---

"The only way to make sense out of change is to plunge into it, move with it, and join the dance."

Alan Watts

For many of us, when we finally get past using porn, we cling to the idea of retaining our sexual energy. The powerful benefits of preserving our sexual energy are so dramatically life changing that it's easy to get completely stuck on preserving ourselves. We feel so great that we would do almost anything to not jeopardize the "achievement" of this powerful state of being. Clinging, if persisted in, can be a major problem that eventually leads right back to porn use.

Let me explain. So here you are, feeling like *A Brand New You.* Powerful, motivated, optimistic, and proud of how far you've come. You feel confident, bold, and ready to take on anything the world throws at you. It's an incredible feeling. You feel like a god compared to your past porn-using self.

It's easy to assume that much of our progress can be attributed to the preservation of our sexual energy. Although this is true in a sense, this assumption can get us into trouble. Because we place tremendous value on the preservation of our sexual energy, it's easy to come to the conclusion that ejaculation is bad. The idea of ejaculation being bad, combined with the feelings associated with a relapse, and it's super easy to avoid ejaculation at all costs.

The avoidance of ejaculation then subconsciously blocks us from forming a meaningful, intimate relationship. This subconscious blocking happens because we associate losing our "achievement" with the expending of our sexual energy by ejaculation through sex. Because this idea lingers in the back of our mind, we then shy away from taking steps toward pursuing an intimate relationship, such as approaching women, or dating altogether. Then, because we avoid pursuing a relationship, a relationship never happens. If a long enough time passes in solitude, we become lonely.

This was one of the biggest challenges that I had to overcome on my journey. I had made so much progress that I didn't want to jeopardize it for anything. Time passed quickly, and before I knew it I was 18 months into my journey of quitting porn. Managing my sexual energy became pretty easy, and in August of 2016, I hit my first full year of porn-free living since deciding to quit.

During the back end of these 18 months, I was so focused on the achievement of my goals, which at the time was becoming a pro golfer on the PGA Tour, that I completely neglected my deep desire to form an intimate relationship. I channeled 110% of my sexual energy into the pursuit of becoming a successful pro golfer. This meant sacrificing many things, among which was the desire to explore the possibility of forming an intimate relationship.

I had made marked progress on my golf game and mastered the control of my sexual desire, but a new problem surfaced; loneliness. Loneliness began to manifest because I was so focused on my goals. I'm obsessive by nature, and felt that the achievement of my goals depended on my ability to continue to retain my sexual energy. Because of this, I lost my healthy life balance. This obsession with my goals then caused me to subconsciously avoid women altogether. I went on dates here and there, but nothing serious developed because I had walls that couldn't be penetrated. I was determined to not let anyone in. I continued to cling to the "achievement" of this new powerful state of being, and I wasn't going to sacrifice that for anything, or so I thought.

This was the perfect storm for relapse. I felt that I had mastered my sexual energy, but I was also very lonely. Because I had such "great" control of my sexual desire, I naively believed that I could satisfy my loneliness, but also preserve my sexual energy, by edging.

In the porn recovery community, edging is the term used for watching porn without ejaculation. I justified edging in order to "preserve" my sexual energy and retain my life gains. It was a cocky idea, and it would eventually bite me in the ass. This edging activity went on for about a week until I inadvertently crossed the point of no return, and blew it.

It hit me hard. Almost two years after deciding to quit using porn, and a full year of being fully porn-free, and here I was; back at square one. I was disgusted with myself. I played with fire, and finally got burnt. This relapse was a slap in the face, and a bitter wake-up call for me.

It wasn't two minutes after this relapse that I recommitted myself to staying off of porn, for good. But this time I knew that I had to adjust my mindset. Yes, my sexual energy was extremely valuable when preserved, but I couldn't allow the idea of retaining it to block me from pursuing an intimate relationship. I vouched to allow myself to re-enter the dating scene, and told myself that it was okay to have sex again.

Time passed, and after having a few romantic encounters, including a girlfriend, I realized that progress and growth doesn't magically disappear after orgasm during sex.

I learned that the disgust and disappointment of relapse is exclusive to porn. Ejaculation during sex doesn't carry the same depressing affect that relapsing to porn does. Sure, you still feel a little tired after orgasm during sex, but you don't incur the subconscious damage and conscious guilt that follows a porn relapse.

However, it's very easy for someone to confuse the feelings of post-relapse with what is felt after orgasm during sex. This misunderstanding is a major block for many men recovering from porn use. The only way to fully understand the difference between sex and porn use is to experience sex for yourself.

The avoidance of the pain associated with a relapse shows just how powerfully destructive porn is on our subconscious minds. The negative impact from porn use is so powerful that we'd do almost anything to avoid that pain again. The avoidance of that pain is a reminder of how serious a problem porn use is, and how important it is to raise awareness and create new resources for those fighting to get their lives back on track.

CHAPTER 36

A New Relationship with Sex | A Tool for Intimacy

"Sex deepens love and love deepens sex, so physical intimacy transforms everything and playing with it is playing with fire."

Merle Shain

Another aspect of quitting porn that's important to talk about is our post-recovery relationship with sex. Whether we realize it or not, porn influences how we view sex. Most of the time the influence is negative. It's very easy, especially for someone who grew up watching porn, to develop unrealistic expectations of what sex is like in real life. Porn use can even lead to the objectification women. You can spot this issue in yourself if you have the desire to act out what you've viewed while watching porn. This ill formed definition of sex can lead to the inability to form and sustain a meaningful romantic relationship. A twisted definition of sex is also emotionally and spiritually harmful to both you and your partner.

As humans, we have an innate desire to connect and be intimate. I believe this connection and intimacy is a crucial component in our development and evolution. That said, an unrecognized misalignment can lead to confusion, isolation, and straight up depression, because of the affect it has on our ability to connect with another person on a deep level. Porn literally blocks us from being able to love fully, and form meaningful intimate relationships, all without us knowing. This all happens below the surface of our conscious mind, which basically leaves us helpless against avoiding it.

I know there are people reading this saying, "I have a girlfriend, and I watch porn. See, you're wrong." And on the surface, it may seem that you're correct. However, how deep of a connection do you really have? How committed are you to your partner? What's the level of intimacy that you share within your relationship? My point is that by using porn you're subconsciously affecting your definition of sex, and because of that there's a next-level of intimacy that you may be missing out on.

I know from experience that porn affected how I viewed sex, and also affected my ability to form and maintain romantic relationships. Porn gave me a superficial idea of what sex should be like, and that idea held me back from reaching the deeper levels of intimacy that I'm referring to. Changing my definition of sex was beyond my control because it was rooted below my conscious awareness. As long as I kept using porn, there was no way I could reshape my idea of healthy sex. The only way to reshape it was to remove porn from my life.

However, the coolest experience was that once I had time off from using porn, my definition of healthy sex changed naturally. Porn dulls out our ability to feel our emotions. If we can't feel deeply into our own emotions, we can't feel deeply into the emotions of others. Our capacity for intimacy depends greatly on this natural ability to feel deeply into both our emotions, and our partner's emotions simultaneously. Once we have time off from using porn, we regain our ability to feel naturally.

As I distanced myself from porn, I began to look at both sex and women differently. I slowly began to recognize my heart's truest desires. These truest desires were for intimacy and deep connection, not surface-level instant gratification.

Many of the men I mentor report this same phenomena. Once they quit porn, their passion for their partner increases, and they deepen their level of intimacy within their relationship effortlessly. Quitting porn brings them closer together. And single men who haven't previously had a desire to pursue intimacy, often realize that they develop this desire once they quit using porn. This new desire for intimacy and companionship lies below the layer of pornographic sexual conditioning that subconsciously affects how they look at sex and love. Once porn is removed, the desire for romantic connection arises naturally.

So as you travel on your journey of quitting porn use, expect a new level of emotional awareness to develop within yourself. Allow these emotions to come up. You might notice a growing desire to connect romantically, or you might just need to have a good cry. Regardless, allow these emotions to arise, and welcome them with gentle non-judgement.

Allow the surfacing of your emotions to happen naturally. Don't resist anything. Depending on how long these emotions have been buried below the surface will influence both the frequency of their surfacing, and the magnitude of their strength. The trend seems to be that the more severe the porn habit, the more impact the surfacing of these emotions have. Just allow them to come up. Eventually, it'll slow down, and you'll attain a healthy emotional balance. As you progress, your idea of sex, intimacy, and companionship will shift in proportion to your time away from porn. You'll no longer see sex as a surface level act, but rather a tool to deepen intimacy and strengthen love.

Quitting porn allows you to develop a new, healthy relationship with sex. This shift opens the door for you to grow into your ability to connect on a deeper level, and form meaningful intimate relationships. Once this door opens for you, the only thing left to do is to step through it, and love fearlessly.

CHAPTER 37

Enjoying the Process of Transformation | Your Ever-Evolving Self

---

"He who lives in harmony with himself,
lives in harmony with the universe."

Marcus Aurelius

The process of self-transformation is a journey that never ends. There never comes a point where we've finally made it. There never comes a point where we can stop focusing on our development. There never comes a point where we can sit back, and be finished.

The art of transformation lies in the ability to enjoy and appreciate the process of continuous change, regardless of whether it feels good or bad. Is it all sunshine and roses? No, it's far from that. In fact, much of the time it feels like there's more struggle than ease. But I always remind myself that we need darkness to appreciate the light. I always remind myself that the freedom lies just beyond the struggle.

Realizing the utility of struggle and the impermanence of everything in life takes the pressure off. Understanding this dampens our drive to be perfect, because perfection is not attainable. We're only able to move through transformation with grace, once we realize that we'll never "arrive" because there's no final destination. The true essence of life is pure change. All we can do is remain committed to bringing the best version of our self into every moment of every day. Everything outside of who we show up in life as is beyond our control.

Our personal evolution has no limits. The only limits we have are the ones we put on ourselves. We can continuously evolve if we choose to. We only stop growing when we choose to stop growing. The steps we take in pursuit of growth on our journey through life are footprints of success. Each step is the progressive realization of our transformation. Every step on our journey plays an important role in our development. In this sense, you're always winning because there isn't a moment in time when you aren't pushing your personal evolution forward.

It's also important to remind ourselves that we each begin at a different point on the spectrum of self-transformation. We all travel different paths on this journey. The one thing we all have in common is our decision to take responsibility for ourselves, and the desire for an awesome life. Stay committed through all of the ups and downs, and you can't lose. We only lose when we give up. We only lose when we quit on ourselves.

By persevering on this journey you'll learn more about yourself than you ever thought was possible. You'll learn about your strengths, weaknesses, what you love, and what you don't love. There'll be times when you don't know what to do and you want to scream at the top of your lungs. Don't worry. Trust the journey. Everything we experience in life is meant to grow us. Every experience we have is perfect for us in that very moment. You'll look back at even the hardest times, and realize that they were thrust upon you for a reason. They were thrust upon you to push you forward. They were thrust upon you to strengthen your resilience, and harden your character. Welcome adversity into your life, because it's in times of difficulty that we learn the most about ourselves.

The essence of self-transformation is nurturing the increasing ability to flow like water through the ever-changing landscape of life. If we fight the current, we make no progress. If we set our sails fearlessly, we flow with the current of the universe, and evolution happens naturally. This is our goal; to flow effortlessly with the current of life, and never look back. For life in this moment will never be the same ever again, and neither will you.

Further Reading

"I am a part of everything that
I have read."

Theodore Roosevelt

This book has been designed to help you think for yourself, and to trigger the pursuit of further learning. I've compiled a list of my favorite books that've helped me on my journey. I hope that you utilize these works of priceless wisdom and powerful insight to expand your knowledge, and your understanding of life.

The Impact of Porn on Your Life

Your Brain on Porn, by Gary Wilson

The Porn Myth, by Matthew Fradd

The Mind

As a Man Thinketh, by James Allen

Thinking for a Change, by John C Maxwell

Think and Grow Rich, by Napoleon Hill

The Spirit

The Power of Now, by Eckhart Tolle

Self-Discipline, Self-Control and Will-Power

No Excuses, by Brian Tracy

The Marshmallow Test, by Walter Mischel

Willpower, by Roy F. Baumeister & John Tierney

Stoicism

The Obstacle is the Way, by Ryan Holiday

Relationships and Love

The Way of the Superior Man, by David Deida

The Mastery of Love, by Don Miguel Ruiz

Social Media, Focus, and Concentration

Deep Work, by Cal Newport

High Performance

Flow, by Mihaly Csikszentmihalyi

Peak, by Anders Ericsson and Robert Pool

So Good They Can't Ignore You, by Cal Newport

Leadership

The 21 Indispensable Qualities of a Leader, by John C. Maxwell

The Leader Who Had No Title, by Robin Sharma

Creativity

inGenius, by Tina Seelig

Steal like an Artist, by Austin Kleon

Show Your Work, by Austin Kleon

Communication Skills

Talk like TED, by Carmine Gallo

Body Language, by Julius Fast

Sports Psychology

Mind Gym, by Gary Mack & David Casstevens

The Champion's Mind, by Jim Afremow

Golf is a Game of Confidence, by Bob Rotella

Golf for Enlightenment, by Deepak Chopra

Floatation Therapy

The Float Tank Cure, by Shane Stott

Entrepreneurship

#AskGaryVee, by Gary Vaynerchuk

Crushing It, by Gary Vaynerchuk

My Influences

"Mentoring is a brain to pick,
an ear to listen, and a push
in the right direction."

John C. Crosby

Birds of a feather flock together. The following is a list of amazing influencers who've impacted me in many positive ways. Some famous, some not. Learning from them has shaped me into the person I am today. If you're interested in learning more about them, search for them on Google, or YouTube.

Logic, Alan Watts, Sadhguru, James Allen, Eckhart Tolle, Steve Jobs, Greg Plitt, CT Fletcher, Elisha Long, Alana Parekh, Eric Delbuono, Tiger Woods, Jack Nicklaus, Arnold Palmer, Gary Player, Joe Rogan, Tony Robbins, Jim Rohn, Brian Tracy, Bobby Jones, Ben Hogan, Esther Hicks, Bob Proctor, Earl Nightingale, Les Brown, Eric Thomas, Wayne Dyer, Steve Weatherford, Jordan Peterson, Eddie Pinnero, Kristin Martin, Rachel Cox, Todd Cieplinski,

Grant Cardone, Gary Vaynerchuk, David Goggins, Tom Bilyeu, and of course- my mom and dad.

Thank you for motivating, inspiring, and educating me. Without your influence, there is no telling where I would be right now.

About the Author

Greg Strattner Jr. is a creator, mentor, entrepreneur, athlete, and best-selling author. Greg has a passion for creating content that positively impacts lives all over the world. He is an avid competitive golfer, fitness enthusiast, and lives in Westfield, Massachusetts with his two golden retrievers, Bella and Jackson.

For more free insightful content, check out Greg's official YouTube channel, ***Your Best Self Now.***

To get to know Greg on a deeper level, check out his official website, **www.gregstrattnerjr.com**

"A man may die, nations may rise and fall, but an idea lives on."

John F. Kennedy

Printed in Great Britain
by Amazon

59573447R10119